AF609310

RAOUL AUGER FEUILLET

For the Further Improvement of Dancing

London 1710

Translated by John Essex

Noverre Press

Published by
The Noverre Press
Southwold House
Isington Road
Binsted
Hampshire
GU34 4PH

ISBN 978-1-906830-03-8

A CIP catalogue record for this book is available from the British Library

For the Furthur Improvement of Dancing,. *A Treatis of Chorography or ye Art of Dancing Country Dances after A New Character,*

In which

The Figures Steps, & Manner of Performing are describ'd, & ye Rules Demonstrated in an Easie Method adapted to the Meanest Capacity.

Translated from the French of Mon^{sr} Feuillet, *and Improv'd wth many additions, all fairly Engrav'd on Copper plates, and a new Collection of Country Dances describ'd in ye same Character*

by Iohn Essex *Dancing Master.*

LONDON.

Sold by I. Walsh & P. Randall *Musical Instrument Makers in Ordinary to her Majesty, in Catherine Street near Somerset House in ye Strand,* I. Hare *at ye Viol & Flute in Cornhill,* I. Culen *without Temple-barr, & by ye Author at his House in Rude-lane Fanchurch-street.* 171[illegible]

To Her Grace the Dutches of Bolton

Madam.

As Every thing that is Curious & Novel at first, stands in need of ye Patronage of some illustrious name to protect it, I have wth all Humble Submission to your Grace made Choice of yours; with this assurance that what ever your Grace is pleas'd to favour ye World will accept, for as all you say & doe is agreable, your Grace can no soner approve of a Performance in an Art in which we all know your Grace has Condesended to Excell, but every body will applaud it, where fore without depending on ye Merits of this Trifle I shall only ask Pardon for ye ambition I have assum'd in laying it at your Graces feet, whose particular goodness & Condesention to all gives me ye vanity to subscribe

Madam

Your Graces most obedient & most Humble Servant

John Essex.

The PREFACE

Every Country has had some Particular manner of Dancing peculiar to it self since ye beginning of the World, but this which we call Country Dancing is originaly the Product of this Nation, and is used in most of the Courts in Europe. it is become a mode of Dancing as being more agreeable & Entertaining to Publick Assemblies, and so easie that their's scarce any body of what Capacity so-ever but is Capable of Learning them, and take pleasure in this Art, I may rather say diversion.

And since Mon^sr. Feuillet has been so kind to his own Country, as to form it into a Character easie to be understood, M^r. Isaac has been equally as Generous to Encourage it here, by putting M^r. Weaver upon the First Translation to whom we are much Indebted to for his Improvement.

I am humbly of opinion it will be no ungratfull Subject to ye Quality and Gentry of this Nation, as well as ye Masters, to have ye Manner of Country Dances made easie pleasent & familiar to them. I present you wth some Country Dances of ye French which are these the Female Saylor; ye Pantomime, Gascone Diligent & Micrime, all the rest are my own Composing.

Elements, or Principles of Chorography.

Each leaf of this book represents ye Danceing Roome. viz: the upper part of the leaf where the Musick stands repre-sents the upper end of ye Roome. the lower part of the leaf repre-sents ye lower end of ye Roome. and the two sides of the leaf repre-sent the two sides of ye Roome.

Having given you thus a notion of the Roome, you must take care in ye practique to hold always exactly ye upper end of the book against ye upper end of the Roome so that whatever Motion you make ye book may never come out of it's naturall Situation.

The Right Side of the Roome.

The lower end of the Roome.

Of the Presence of yᵉ Body.

The Body of Man is repre-
-sented by the figure A.B.C.D.
A. shews yᵉ fore part B.
shews the back part and
C.D. the two sides.......

A
C D
B

The Body of the Woman is repre-
-sented as that of yᵉ Man with this
difference that it has a small
half moon more as you
may see by yᵉ figure E.F.G.H.

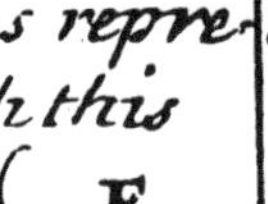

E
G H
F

How the Body is repre-sented over against the four sides of the Room.

The figure I. represents yᵉ Body
against yᵉ upper end of yᵉ Room
The figure K represents yᵉ Body
agˢᵗ yᵉ lower part of the Room
The figure M. represents yᵉ
Body agˢᵗ yᵉ right side of yᵉ Room
and the figure L. represents
the Body against the left
side of the Room.

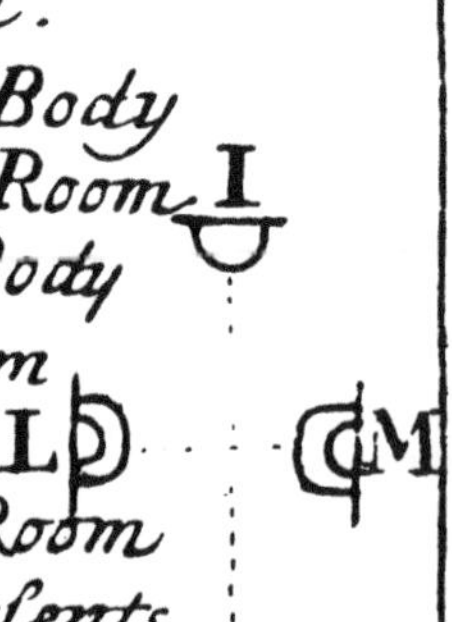

I
L M
K

The left side of the Room.

The lower end of the Room.

Of the Figures of Dances.

The figures of Dances are represented by lines, which begin from y^e presence of the Body, & which goe somtimes forward, & somtimes backward, somtimes sideways to ye right, and somtimes sideways to ye left, either straight or round, but one must observe exactly from whence those lines begin for some of them begin from the fore part of y^e presence of y^e Body, & some from y^e back part, & the other from the sides.

Those that begin from y^e fore part of the presence of the Body, are to goe forward as the line A. shews .... A.

Those that begin from the back part are to goe backwards as the line B. shews .... B

Those that begin from y^e right side are to goe sideways to the right as y^e line C. shews .. C.

Those that begin from y^e left side are to goe sideways to the left as y^e line D. shews .... D.

Examples of all the Different Lines hithertoo mention'd.

line to goe forward and round to the left.

line to goe straight forward.

line to goe forward and round to the right.

line to goe backward and round to the left.

line to goe straight backward.

line to goe backward and round to the right.

line to goe to the left.

line to goe to the right.

line to goe sideways to the left and round.

line to goe sideways to the right and round.

How with the Signes you may form what figure of Dance you please as the figure A.B.C.D. shews which I give here for an Example.

The line A. as I have already said is to goe straight forward.
The line B. is to goe sideways to ye right
The line C. is to goe straight backward.
The line D. is to goe round forward.

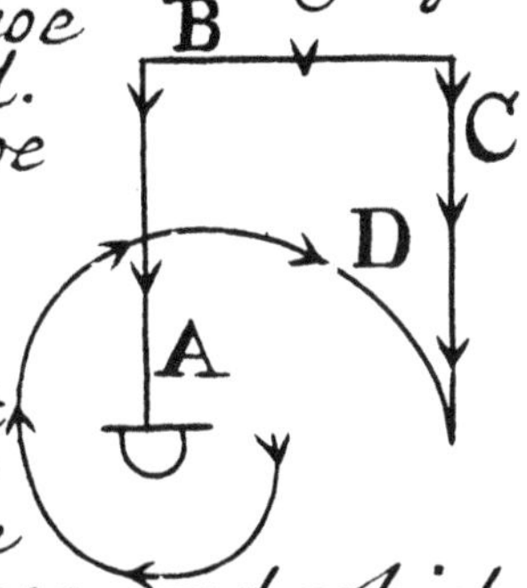

Observe for greater facility that the small Characters which you see from distance to distance, and which are made like small Vs mark the situation of the Body, as it moves as also the presence of the Body which is always at the beginning of every figure of a Dance, and you must likewise observe that it is the upper part of the V. that shews the forepart of the Body.

These small Vs will serve also to mark the measures of ye Dances as will be shewn hereafter.

D A B

Of the Pointed Line.

The pointed line (upon which one doth not goe & which represent no figures of a Dance) serves cheifly to leade the sight from one line to another, as when you will come back upon y^e same line, on which you have gone already.

Example

To goe straight forward & come back on the same line.

To goe sideways and come back on the same line.

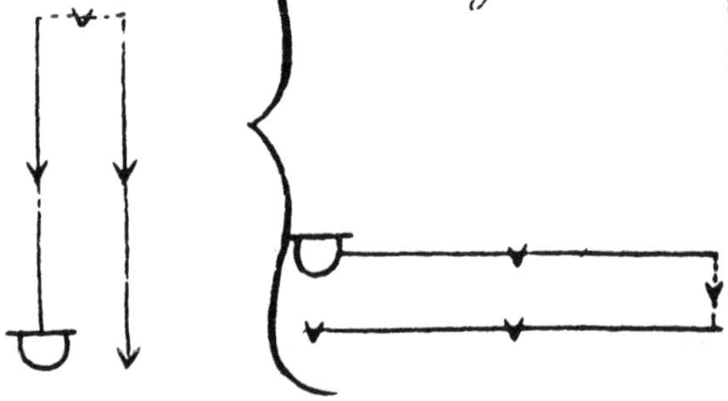

A Pointed line is that also upon which will be placed all Motions of Hands, and Feet and other signes, which are done in y^e same place as will be seen hereafter.

Of yͤ Feet, steps, Hands & Armes.

Tho' my designe is not to mark any steps in Country Dances, being willing to leave the Dancers yͤ liberty of composing the same as they please; there are notwithstanding some motions with yͤ Feet, Hands & Armes which I can't omitt incerting here.

The Foot is represented by the figure A.B. of which A. shews yͤ Heele & B. the Toe. . . . .

The step is represented by the figure C.D. of which C. shews the beginning and D. the end.

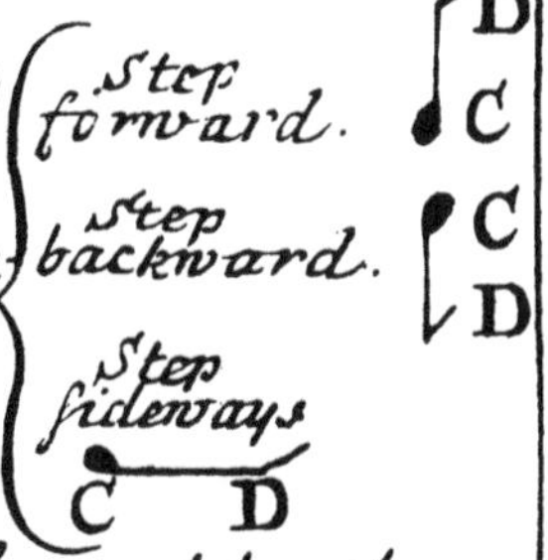

The Hand is represented by the figure E.F. of which E. shews yͤ Thumb and F. yͤ fore finger.

The Arme is represented by the figure G.H. of which G. shews the shoulders and H. the Wrist.

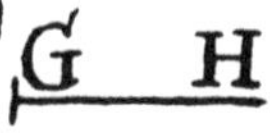

Of the Motions of the Hands, and Feet, and other Signes.

Tis to be observ'd that the lines serve not only to denote y^e figures of Dances, but likewise for a foundation to describe all Motions of the Hands and Feet and other figurs, observing that all what is mark'd at the right side of ye line is always either right Hand, or right Foot, as also that all what is mark'd at the left side is always either left Hand or left Foot.

Example.

To Stamp once with ye Toe upon the Ground.........

Stamp once the Heele upon the Ground.........

Stamp once the flat of the Foot upon ye Ground.

Stamp three times the Toe upon the Ground.........

Stamp three times the Heele upon the Ground.....

Stamp three times the flat of ye Foot upon the Ground.

To walk one step forward and stamp y Ground with the flat of the Foot as in fencing ....

Give the Hand to the Person you Dance with. ....

Let goe the Hand ....

Give both Hands ....

Let goe both Hands .....

Strike with the Hand that is presented ....

Clap both Hands together once

Clap both Hands togather three times ....

Make sign with the finger once as threatning ....

Make sign with the finger three times as threatning ..

Make sign with the finger once as to bid one come ....

Make sign with the finger three times as to bid one come ....

Turning ye Wrist once

Turning ye Wrist three times

Turning both Wrists once

Turning both Wrists three times as when you wind thread

Bend both Knees

Rife on both Feet

Iump on both Feet

Turn to ye right on both Feet a quarter of a turn

Turn to the left on both Feet a quarter of a turn

Turn to the right one both Feet half a turne

Turn to ye left on both Feet half a turn

Iump on both Feet turning a quarter of a turn to ye right

Iump on both Feet turning a quarter of a turn to yᵉ left

Iump on both Feet turning half a turn to the right

Iump on both Feet turning half a turn to the left

A bended ſtep

A riſen ſtep

A bended & riſen ſtep

A ſtep upon the Legg that moves or a bound

A step before you put the Foot upon the Ground, or a hopp ----------------	
Balancing with yͤ right Foot	
Balancing wͭʰ. yͤ left Foot	
A Rigadoon step upon the line forward --------	
A Rigadoon step upon the line backward ------	
Honour to yͤ left Viz. steping sideways with yͤ left Foot & drawing the right Foot behind ----	
Honour to yͤ right Viz. steping sideways with the right Foot and drawing the left Foot behind --------	

How the Measures of Dances, have relation to the Measures of Airs.

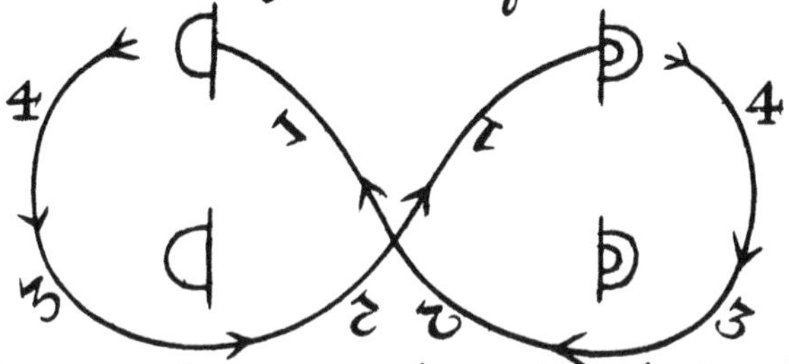

ne must remember that it has been aid heretofore, that ye small V.s which re marked on the figures of Dances, epresent not only the presence of ye ody, when it moves, but that they kewise serve to mark ye measures & ave the same effect in Dances as bars ave in Musick, as may be seen by ye gure above which I give for an example, which figure is of 4 measures like he Aire that is set down on ye top f this leaf, which is also of 4 measures. he first of which has relation to he first measure, of the Dance the 2d. o the 2d. of the Dance. &c.

To know when you must let pass some measures of the Aire with out Dancing, as when two or more persons goe one after another.

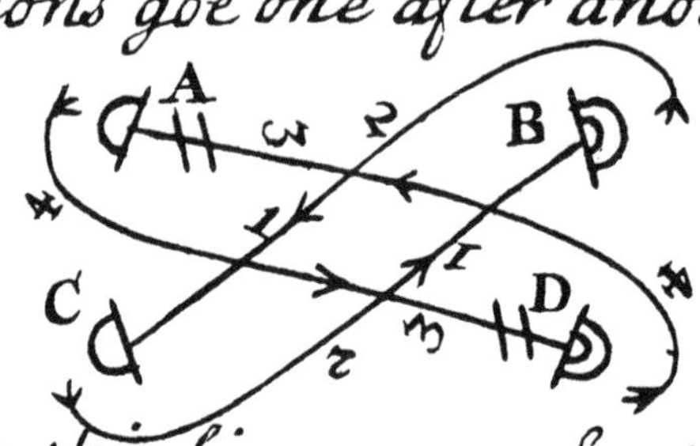

In this figure representing by four persons mark'd A.B.C.D. you must observe that ye two lines A.and D.in their beginning are cut obliquely each by two small barrs, which shews that those two persons, must not begin before they have lett pass two measures of ye Aire, and if there be a greater or smaler number it must be observ'd in proportion.

This being thus known I say that the two persons B.& C.who have no measures to count, must begin presently while ye two other persons A.& D.count two measures after they begin in their tune.

Advice concerning ye steps that best sute with Country-Dances.

The most ordinary steps in Country Dances (those excepted that are upon Minuet Airs) are steps of Gavot, drive sideways Bouree Step and some small Iumps forward of either Foot in a hopping manner; or little hopps in all round Figures as the preeceding & following are, one may make little hopps or Bouree steps but little hopps are more in fashion

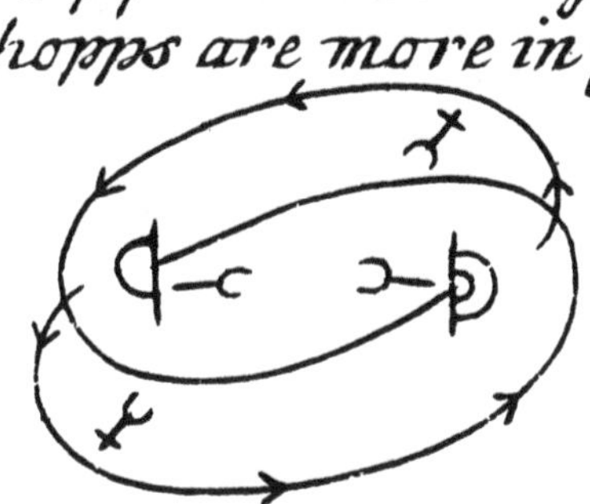

As it is ordinary that every figure of a Dance ends at every cadence or end of the Aire, it will be proper to make a small Iump upon both Feet.

In all figures that goe forwards, and backward, or backwards, and forwards, you must always make Gavott steps.

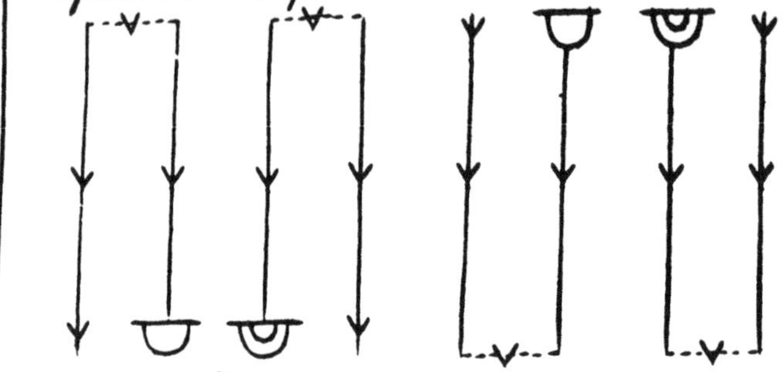

In all figures that goe sideways you must always drive sideways.

Example

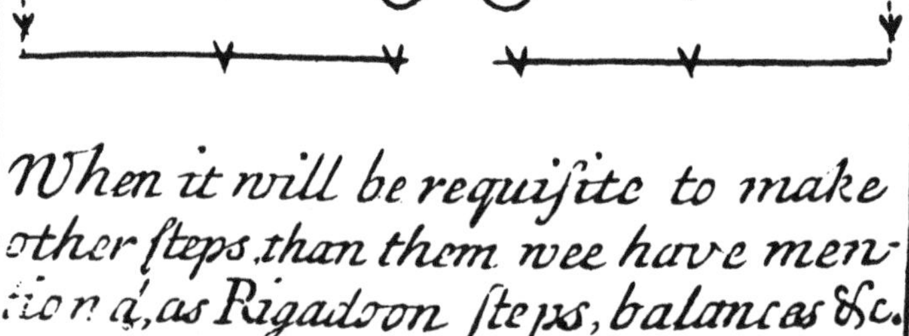

When it will be requisite to make other steps than them wee have mention'd, as Rigadoon steps, balances &c. they shall be mark'd upon ye figures.

What Country Dances are, & how they must be perform'd.

A Country Dance is nothing but a Couplet or partners of a Dance, always repeated, first by two, by 4. 6. 8. 10. &c. and at last by as many Couples as the number of People amounts too.

I call Couple the Man and the Woman that figure togather.

A Couplet in Country Dances is a certain quantity of figures, that fill up the tune.

The same Country Dance may have severall Couplets or parts, wh.ch are like severall verses of Songs upon the same tune.

Each Couplet of a Country Dance is devided by figures viz. first figure 2.d fig: 3. fig: 4.th fig: 5.th fig: &c.

The first figure is always that by which one begins, and goes on till you arrive to ye last, which will be the end of ye part, which is to be repeated not only by them who have begun, but also by all the other Couples.

who must follow the same way as the first, and shall likewise continue in ye same order; till every Body be arriv'd to the same place from whence they begun and then the whole part will be intierely finish'd, and there every Couple make their Honour as they finish.

But if there be a second part, you must instead of making your Honour, goe on in the same order, as you have done in the first, and putt off making your Honour till you come to ye end of the last part.

Country Dances are Danced with as many Persons as you please, provided it be an even number, I mean as many Men as Women, placed upon two lines the Men on one side & ye Women on ye other, of which all ye Couples ought to be distingushed viz. first Couple, 2d. 3d. 4th. 5th. 6th. Couple &c.

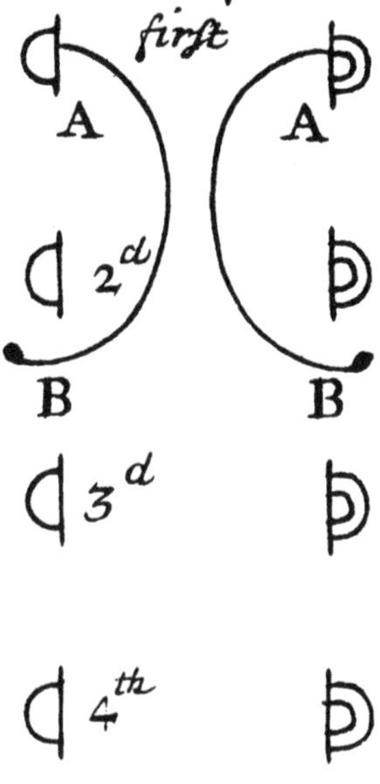

As it wou'd be very difficult for me to mention all figures that Compose a Country Dance, and that it wou'd occaſion too much trouble, I'le content my ſelf for brevity ſake, and to make the thing more eaſie, & give one only for an Example as you may ſee from A. to B. wherein I ſuppoſe that all ye reſt is comprehended, & which I look upon as an abridgm.^{t} to all ye figures that Compoſe a Country Dance.

Example
first
A A
2^d
B B
3^d
4th

There are two cheif Deſigns of Country Dances, upon which all the different figures that may be invented are founded.

The firſt deſign is, that every perſon whatever figure he makes, ends all ye repetitions to the ſame ſide, that is to ſay that ye Man muſt not change his place but wth. another Man, & a Woman but with a Woman.

The Second design is, when ye Men end all their repititions in ye Womens places, and the Women in the Mens places.

In the first design there are four things to be observ'd.

1st When a Couple have begun to Dance, they must not give off till they are come down to the last Couples place as from A. to D.

2d Every repitition must begin always at the first Couple A. & end at the Second Couple B. then to the third Couple C. to the fourth D. &c. and so to come down from Couple, to Couple till you arrive to the last Couple, where then all ye repetitions of ye last Couple are at an end, & that Couple Dances no more but when other Couples coming down, in their turn they move up.

3d That a Couple ought not to begin to Dance, till they're come into the first Couples place, as in A.

4th That a Couple that is come to ye first Couples place must not begin to Dance, till ye precedent Couple has made two repetitions before as from A to C.

Demonstration of the First Design of Country Dances.

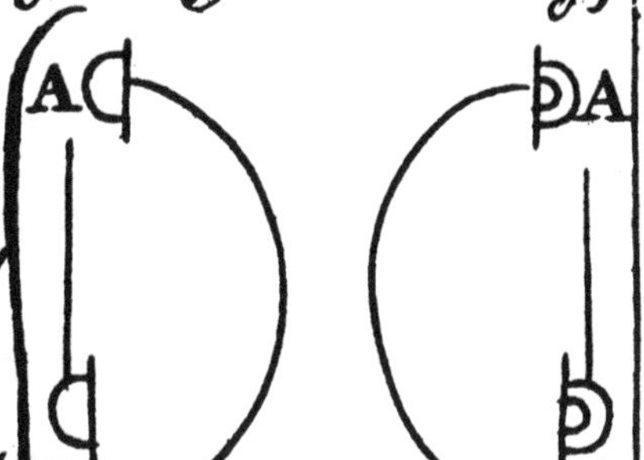

Observe also that every time that a Couple ends their repetition under another Couple, the Couple that is above must move up and take ye place of them that goes down.

A A
B B
C C
D D

In the second design there are also four things to be observ'd.

1.st When a Couple begins to Dance from what-ever place they begin they must not discontinue till they are arriv'd not only to ye last Couples place, but also to ye very place where they have begun

2.d Every time that a repetition begins again, the same increases always by Couples, so that ye Dance which before was but of two, coms to be of four, then of 6. of 8. 10. &c. till every Body be in motion.

3.d When a Couple coms into the first Couples place they must follow the same way which the preceeding Couples have gon.

4.th When a Couple is come down to the last Couple and finds there no Body more to Dance with, then that same Couple Dances again together and afterwards moves up always Dancing, till they come to the same place where they have begun, & then all the repetitions of that Couple are at an end.

Demonſtration of the Second deſign of a Country Dance.

When there is two or more parts in a Country Dance, you'l find the same mark'd one upon another and they will be devided by a barr a cross, of which ye uper one shall be ye first, the next ye second, and the under one ye third, as you may see in ye Country Dance, call'd ye Diligent which has two parts, & the Pantomime which has three.

Whereas Right Hand & left being very difficult for ye Reader to explain at first view, especialy if it be above three quarters round, I shall (therefore) for the greater ease of the Reader, write down in the middle of ye figure, how often you ought to Right Hand, and left the figure, that is mark'd down for three quarters round, as you'l find in ye Great Turk, but if Right Hand and left happen to be done once and a halfe round or more, I shall only in the Character (to avoid Confusion) write downe as before and in words specify how often you are to Right Hand and left.

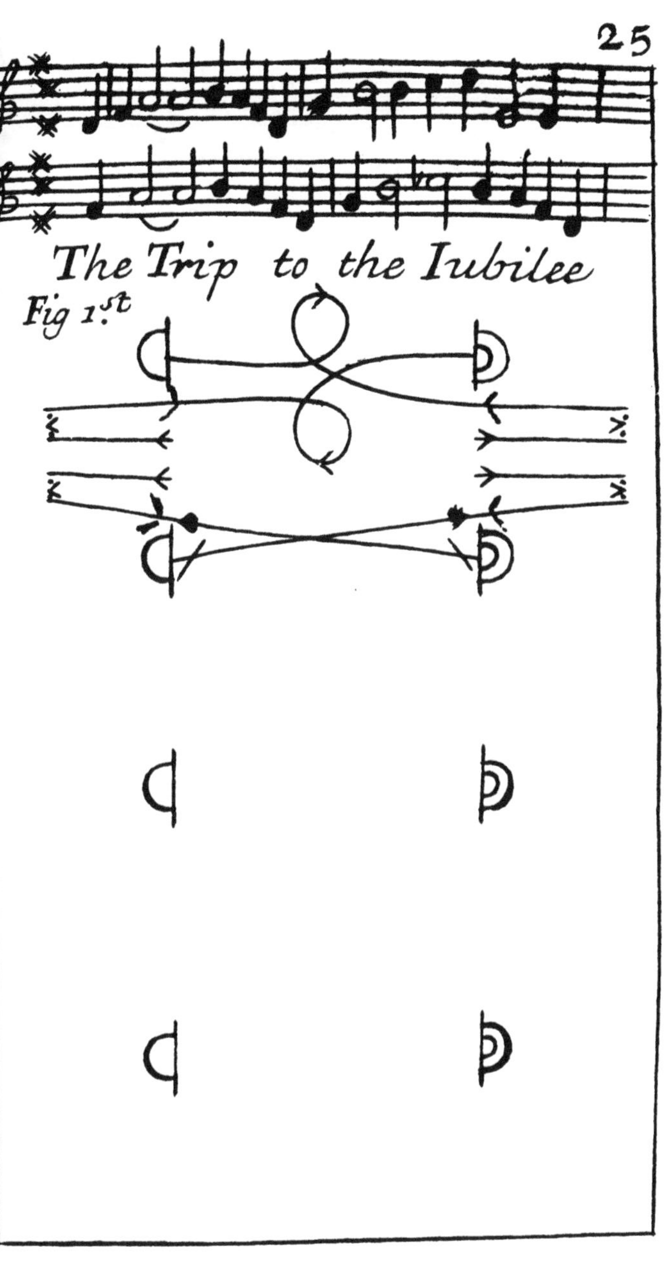
The Trip to the Iubilee
Fig 1.st

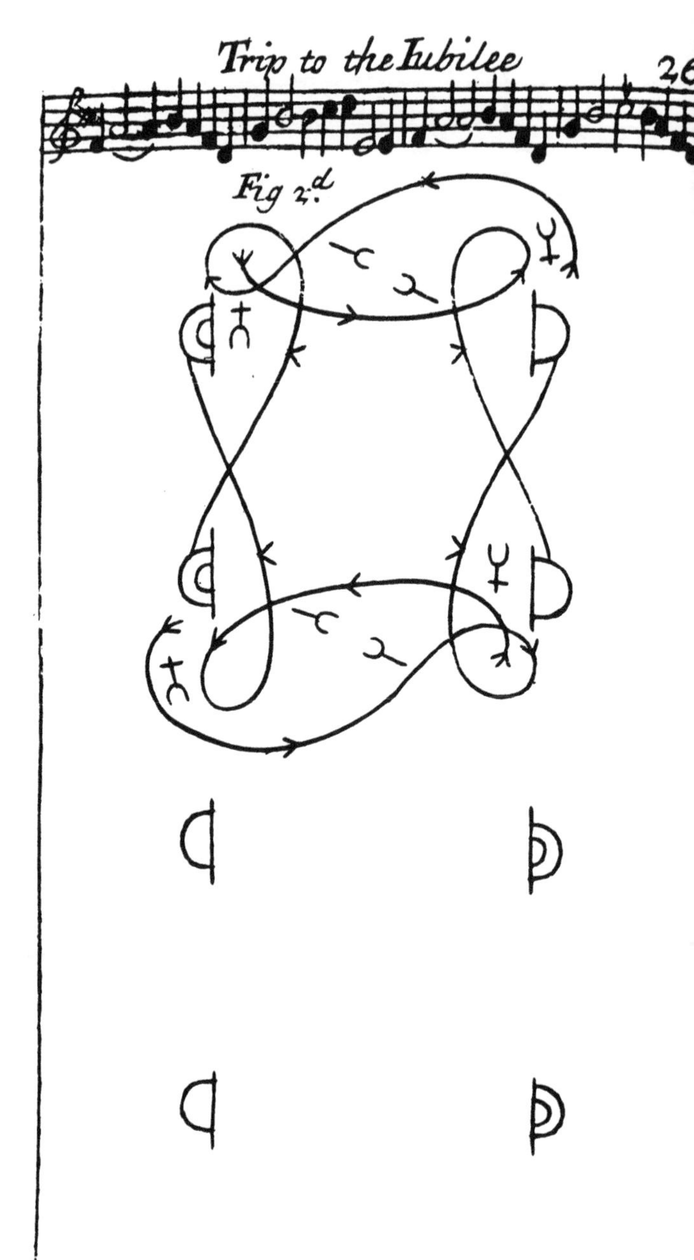
Trip to the Iubilee
Fig 2.d

Trip to the Iubilee

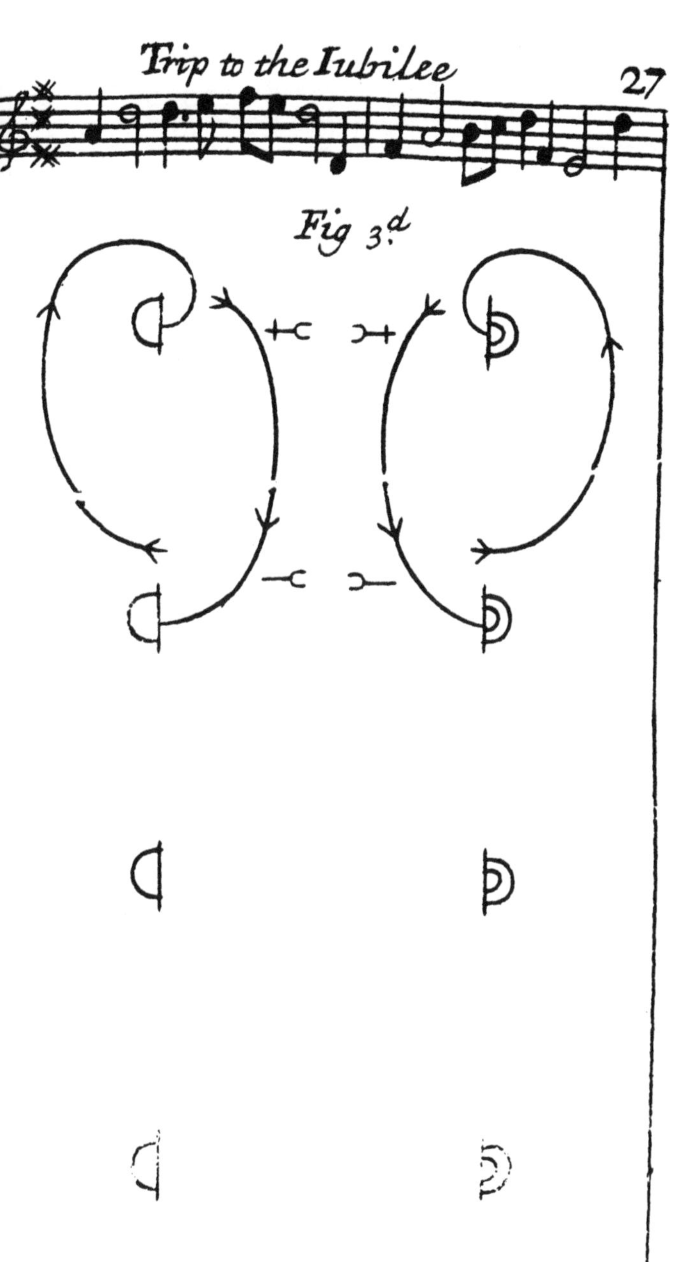

Trip to the Iubilee

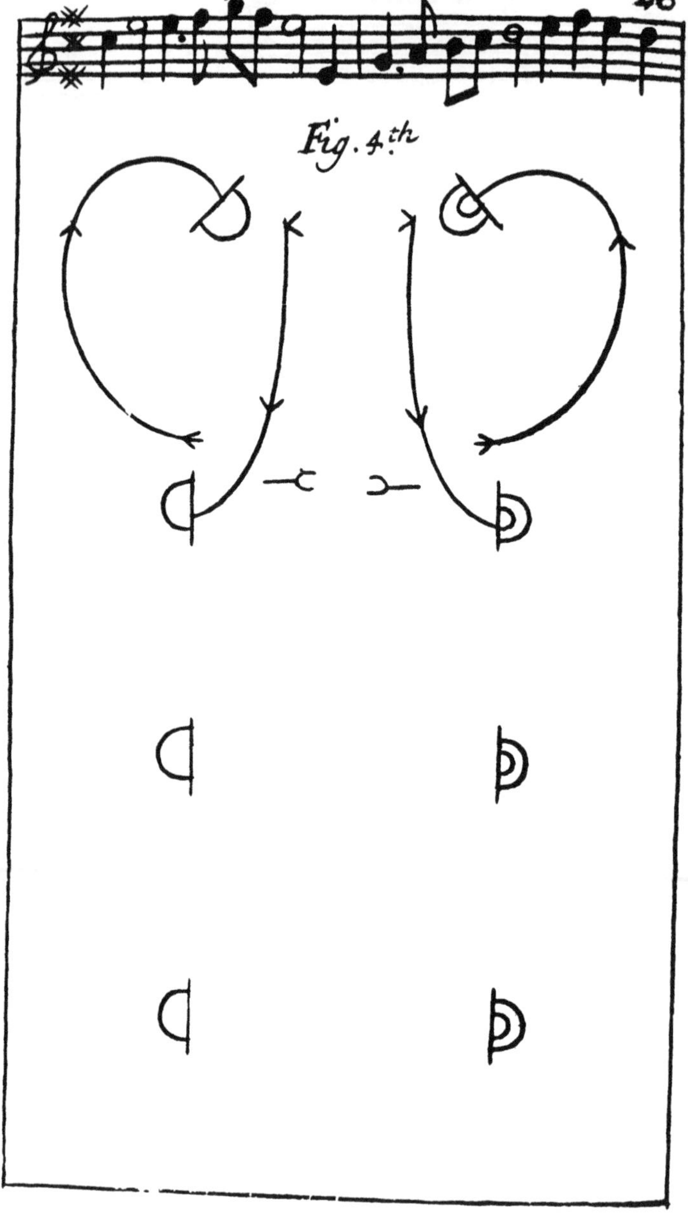

Fig. 4th

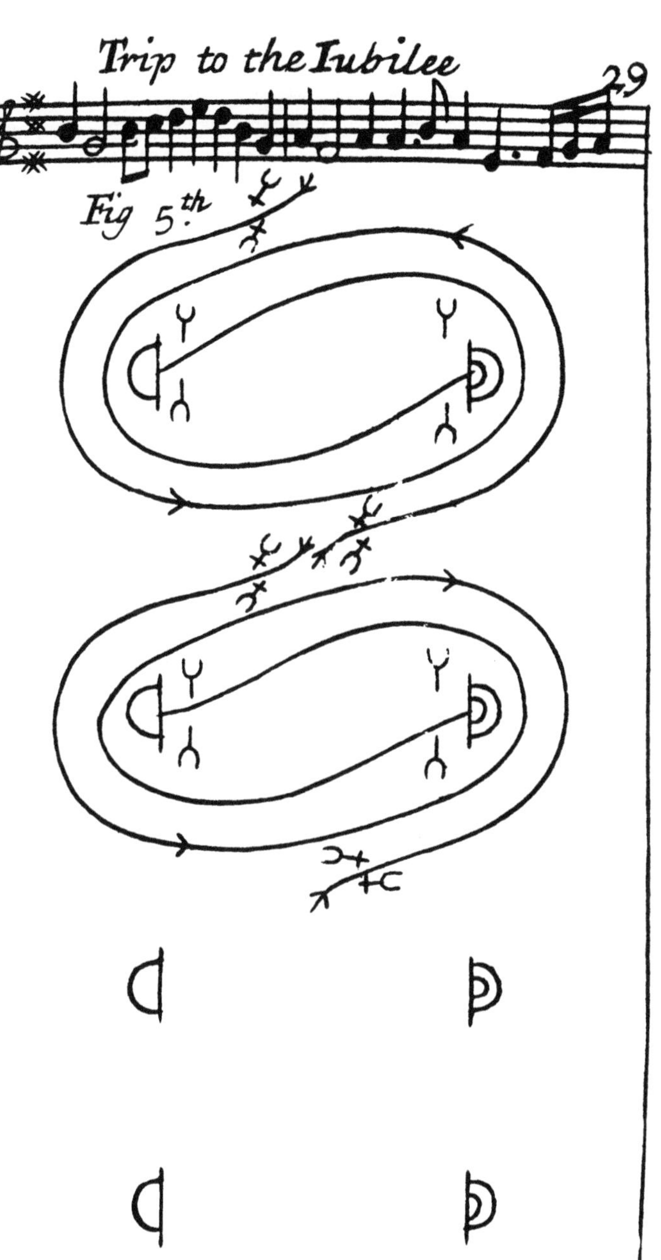
Trip to the Iubilee
29
Fig 5th

Trip to the Iubilee

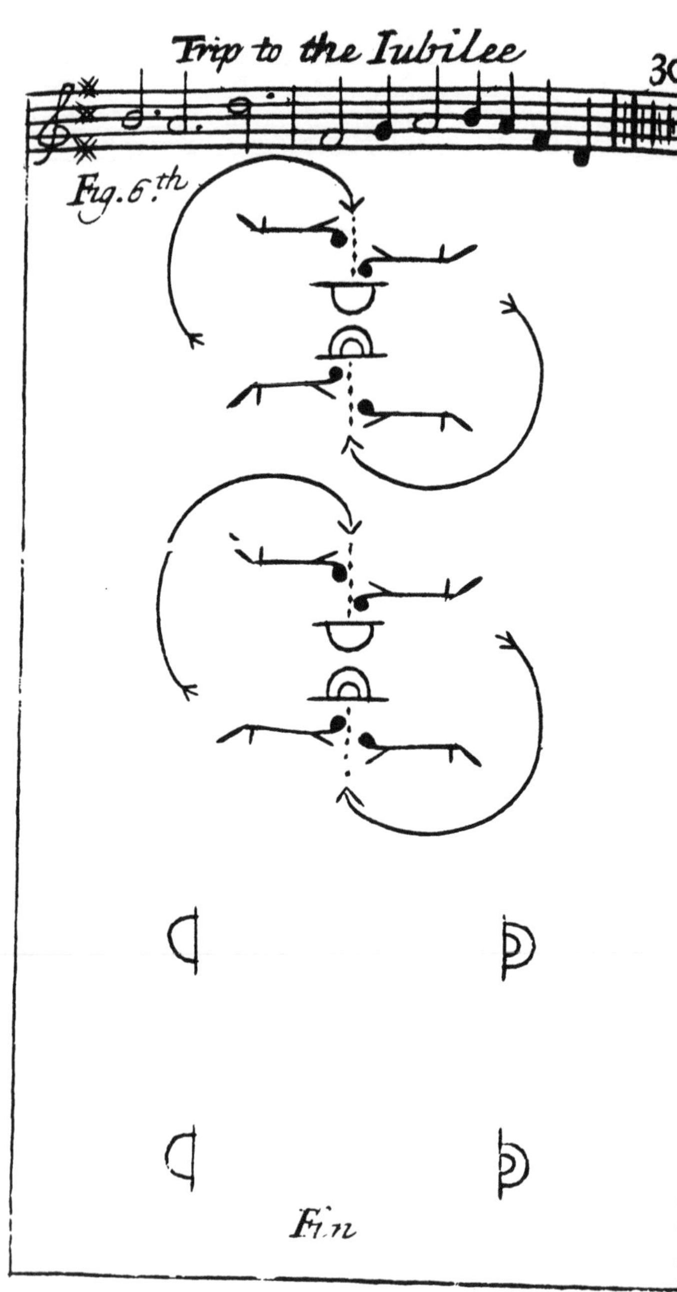

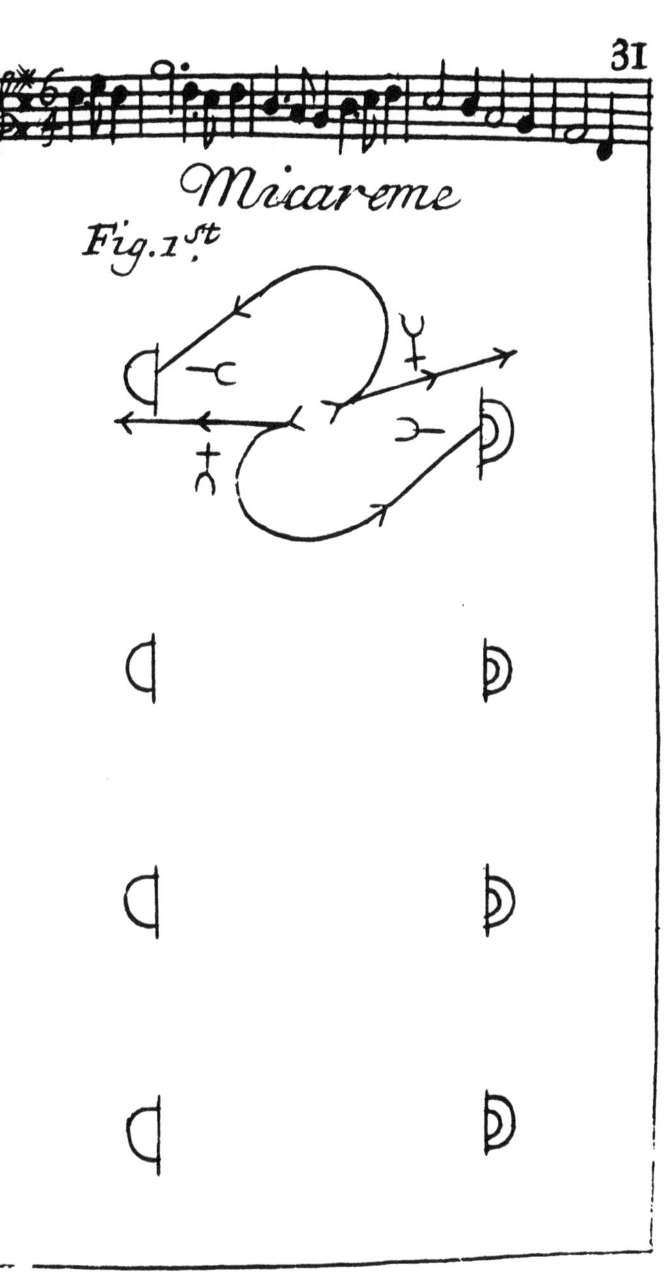
Micareme
Fig. 1.st

Macar'eme

Fig 2.d

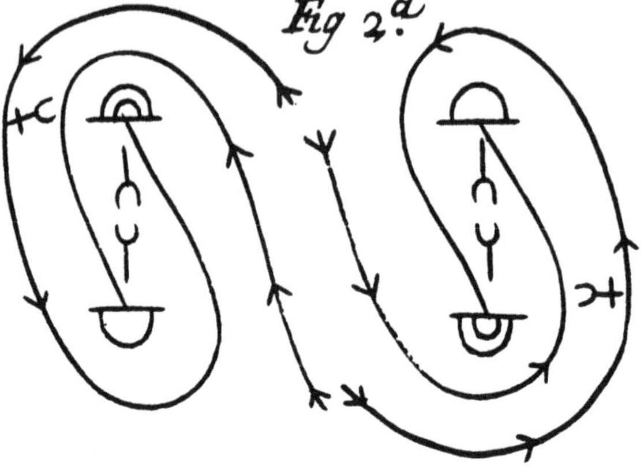

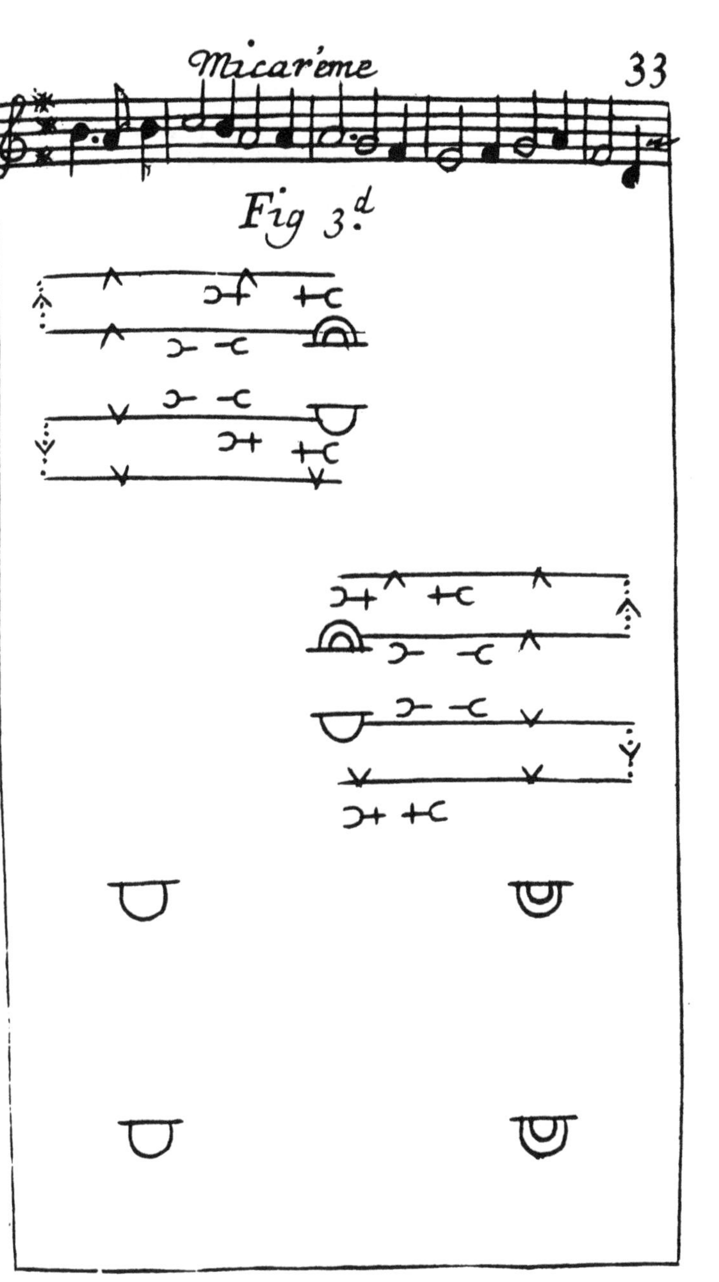
Micarême
Fig 3.d

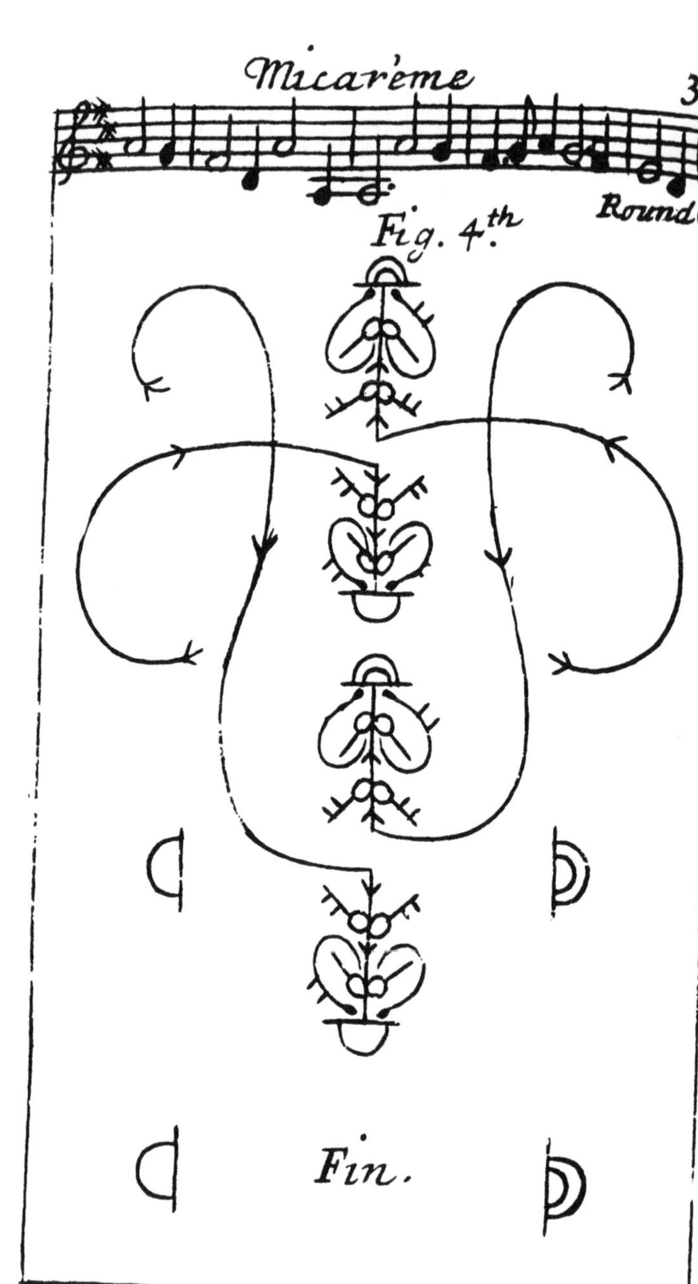
Micarème
Roundo
Fig. 4th.
Fin.

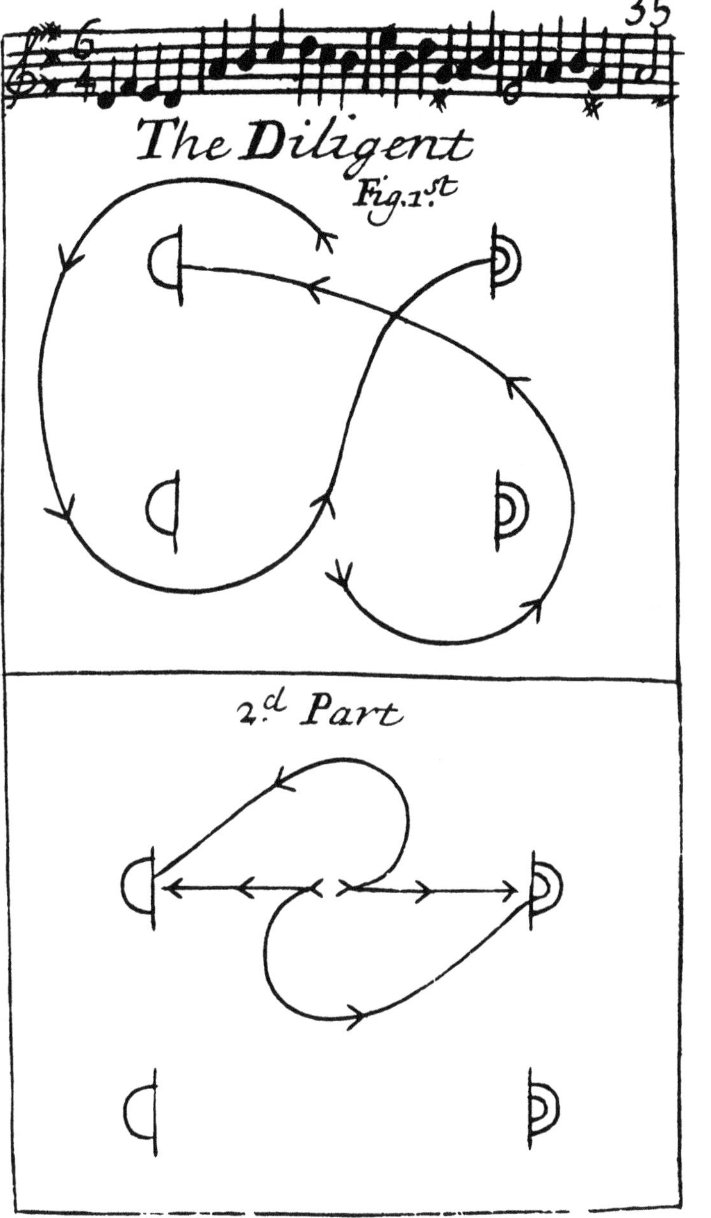
The Diligent
Fig. 1st
2d Part

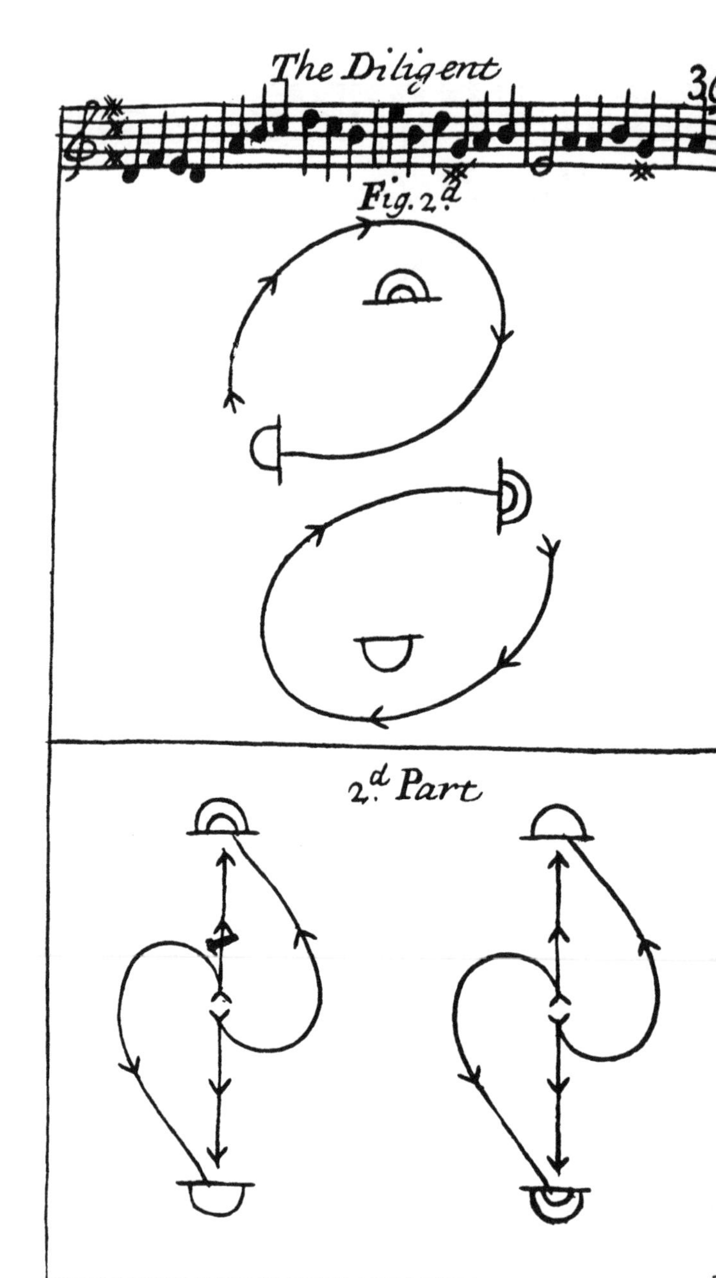
The Diligent
36
Fig. 2.d
2.d Part

Fig. 3.d

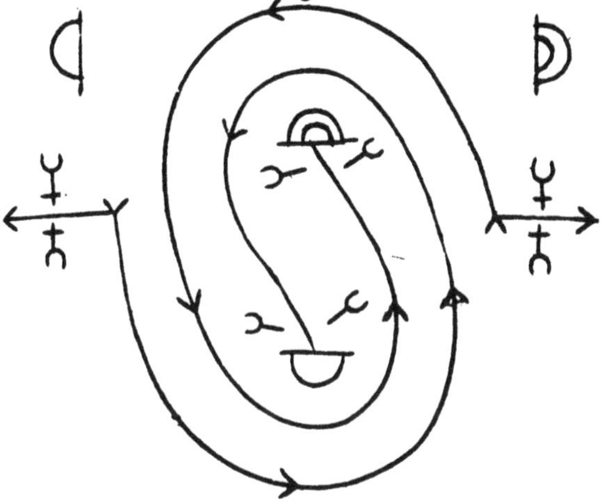

2.d Part

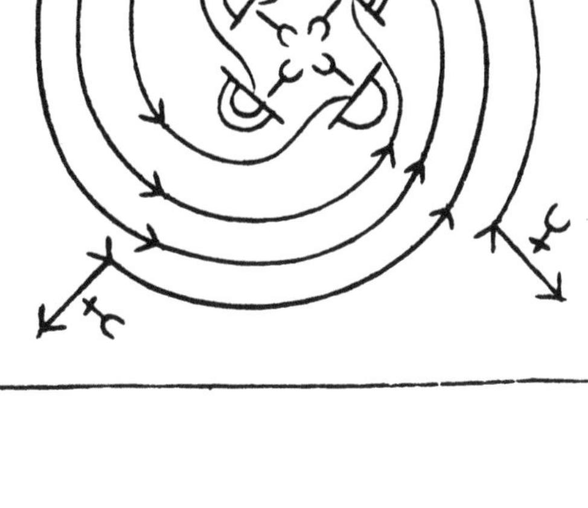

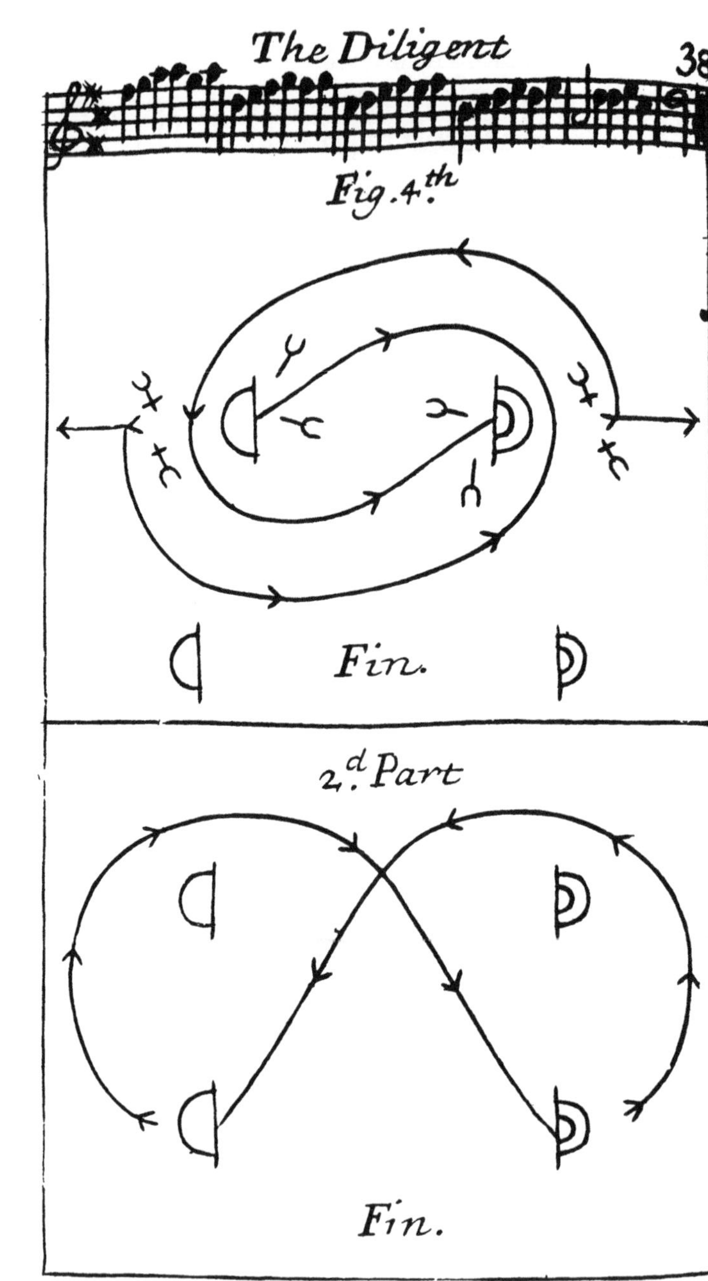
The Diligent
Fig. 4th.
Fin.
2d. Part
Fin.

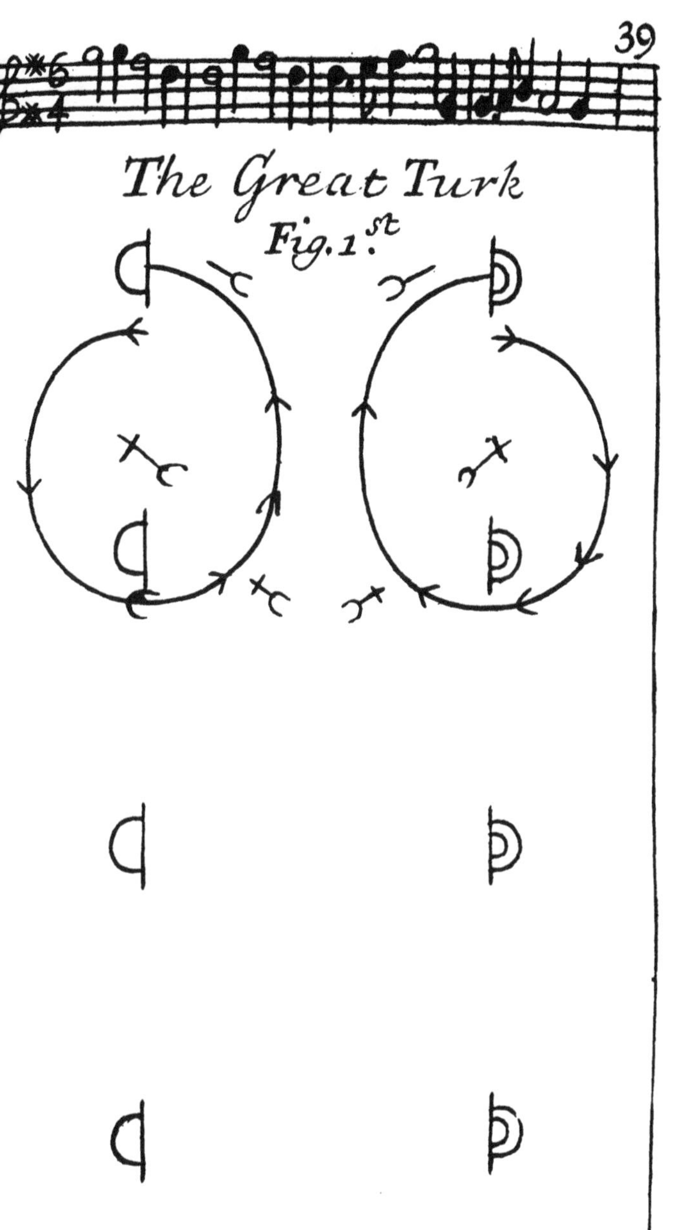
The Great Turk
Fig. 1st

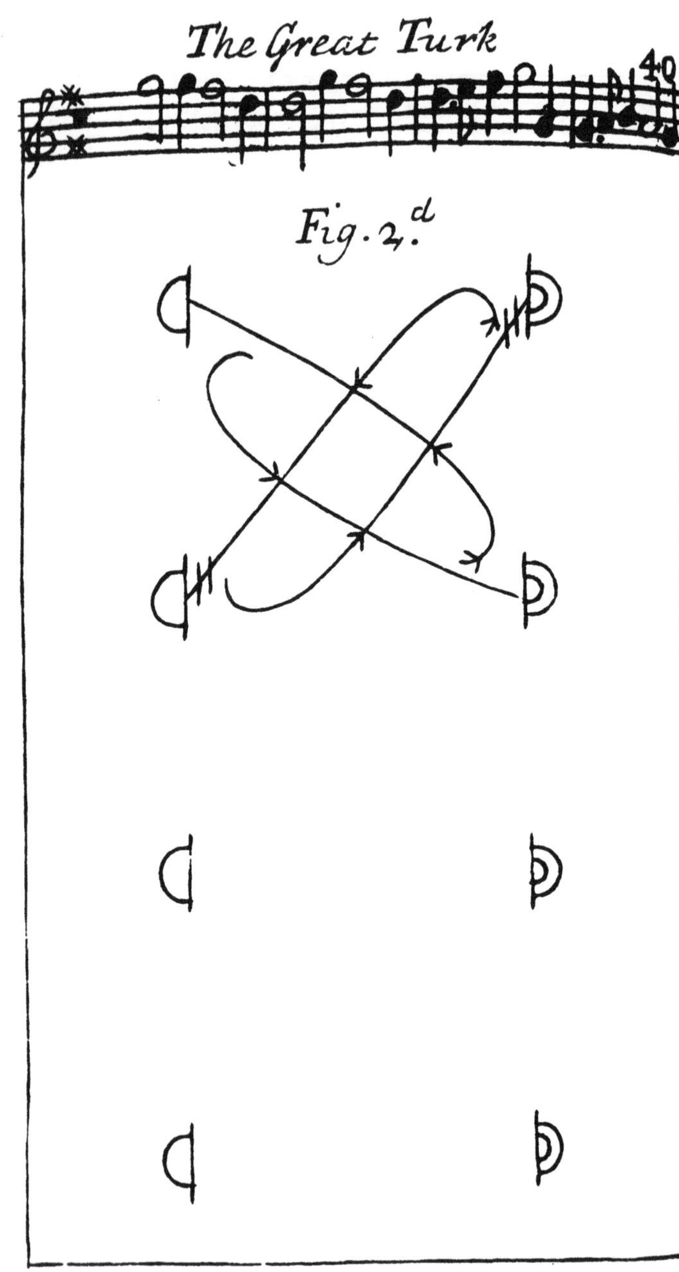
The Great Turk
40
Fig. 2.d

Fig. 3d.

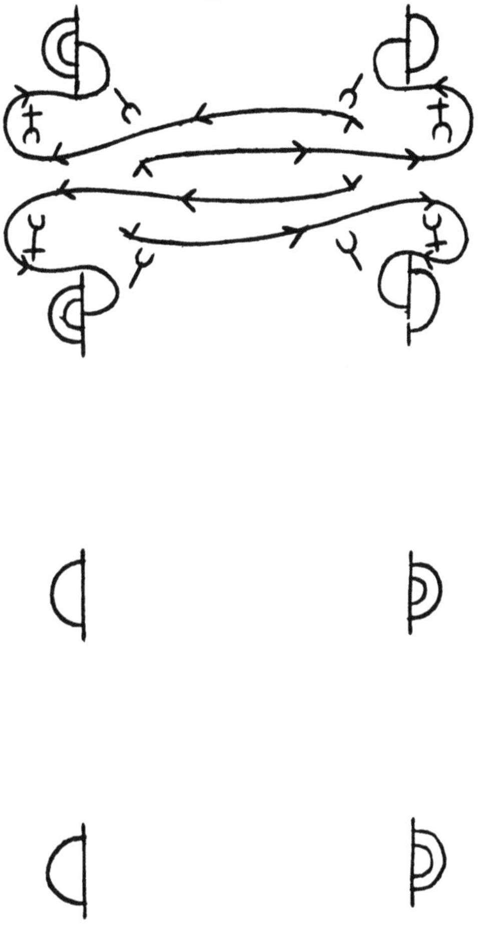

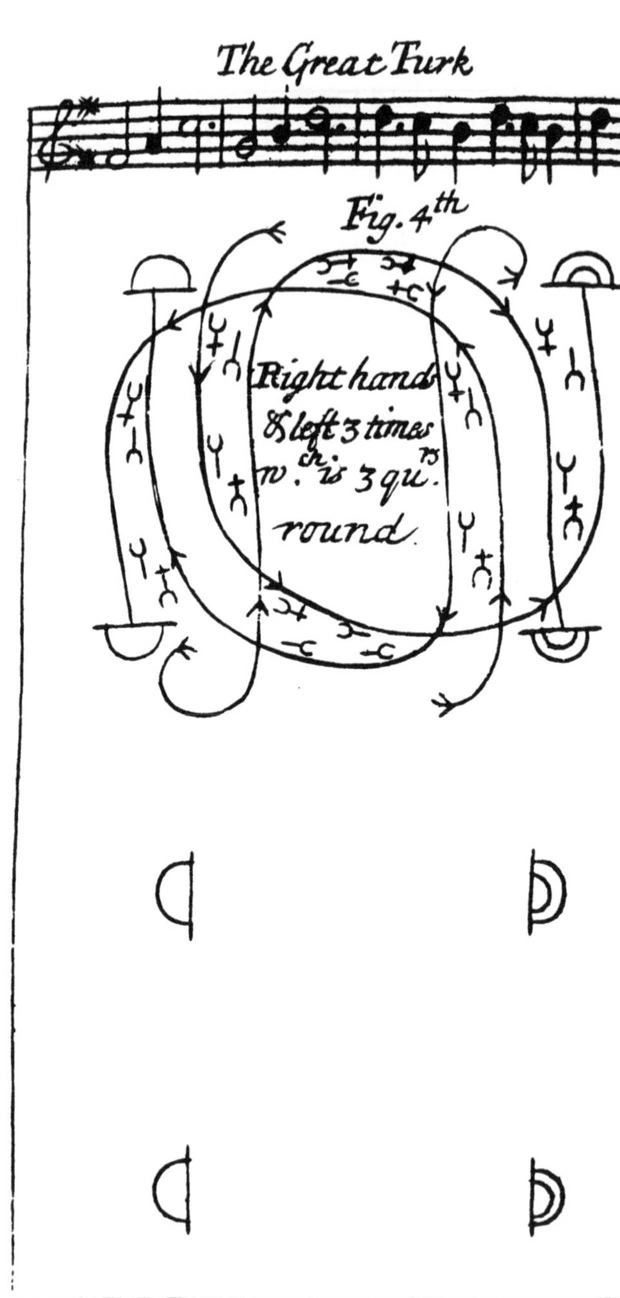
The Great Turk
Fig. 4th
Right hand
& left 3 times
w.ch is 3 qu.rs
round

Fig. 5.th

Fin.

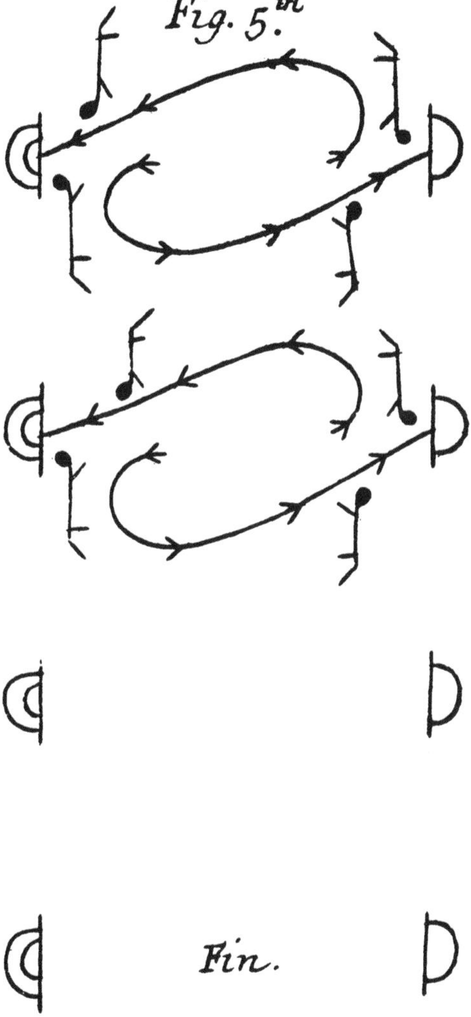

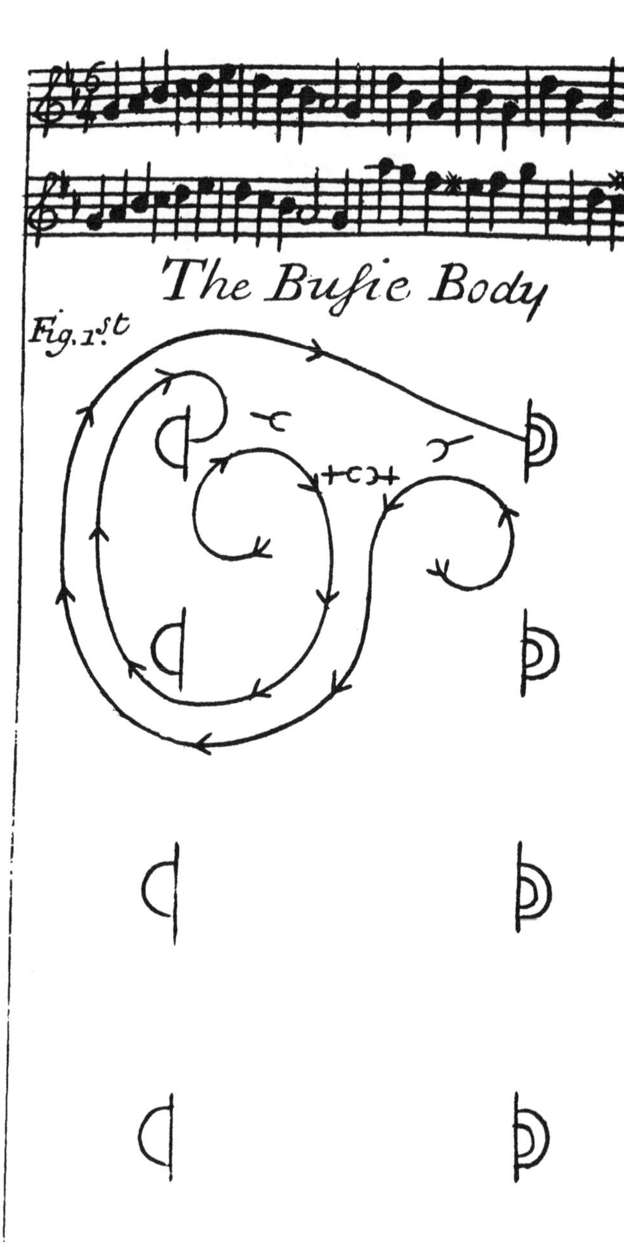
The Busie Body
Fig. 1st

Fig. 2.d

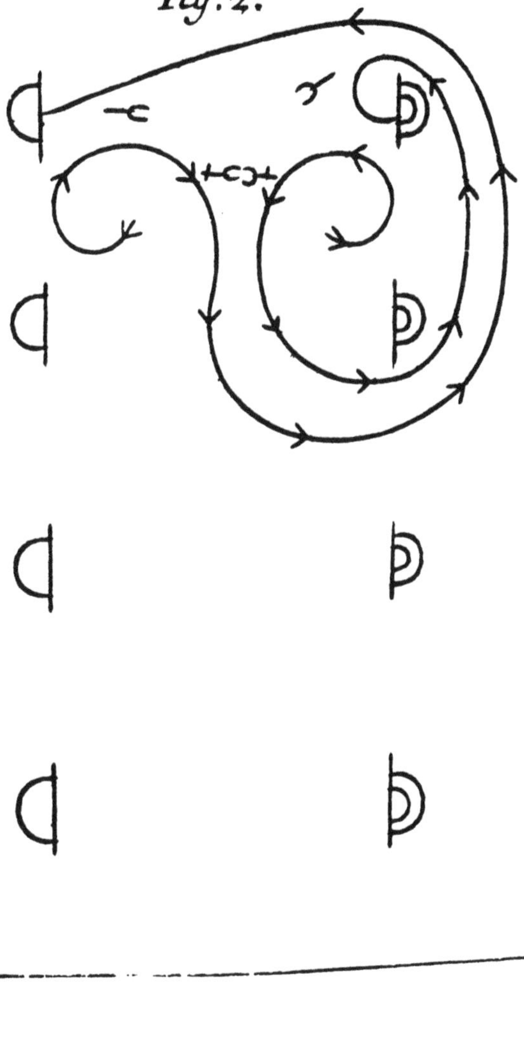

The Busie Body

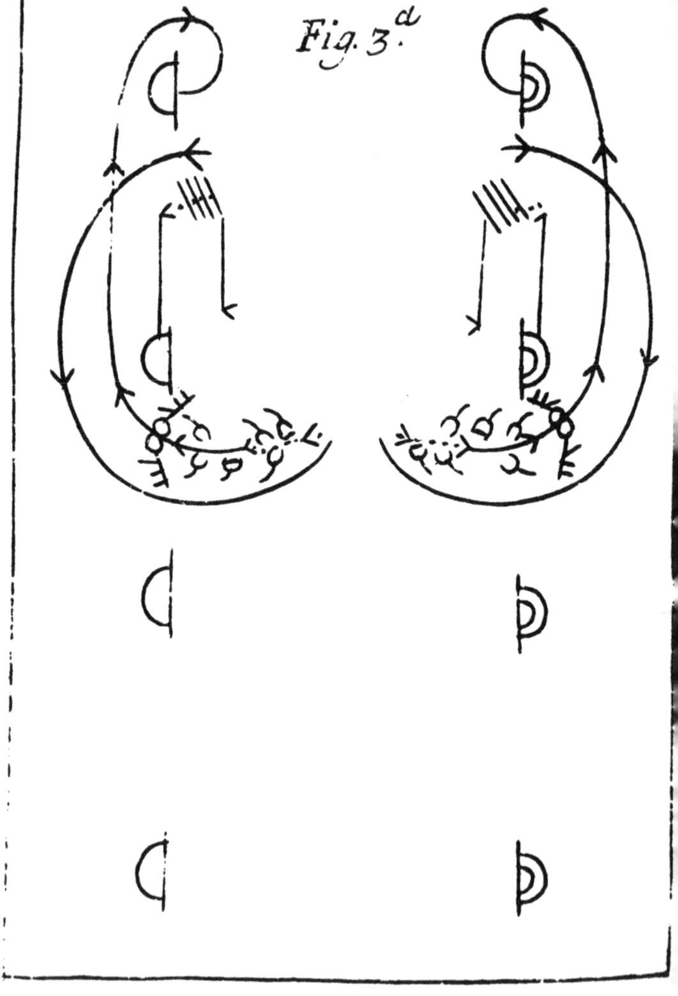

Fig. 3.[d]

The Busie Body

Fig. 4th.

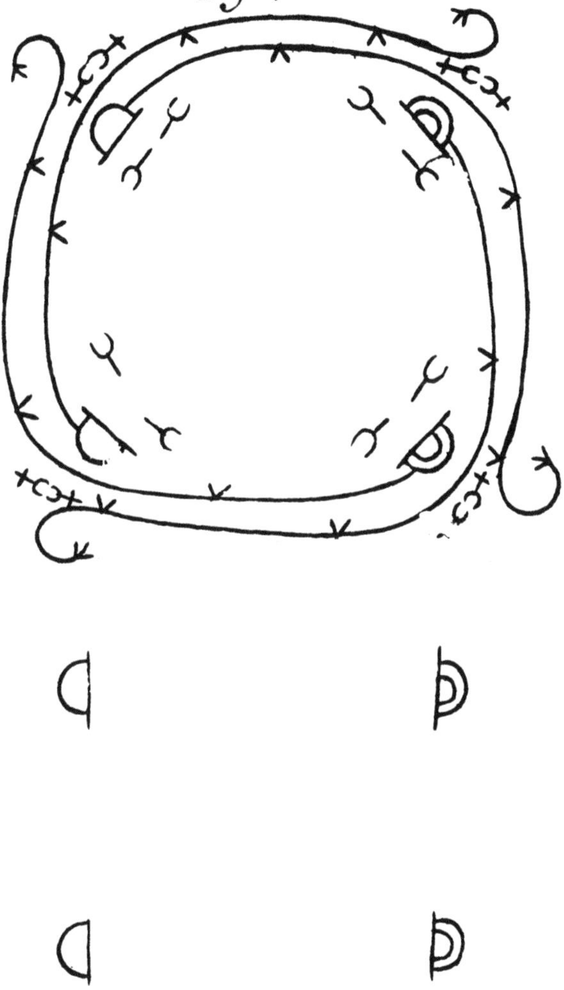

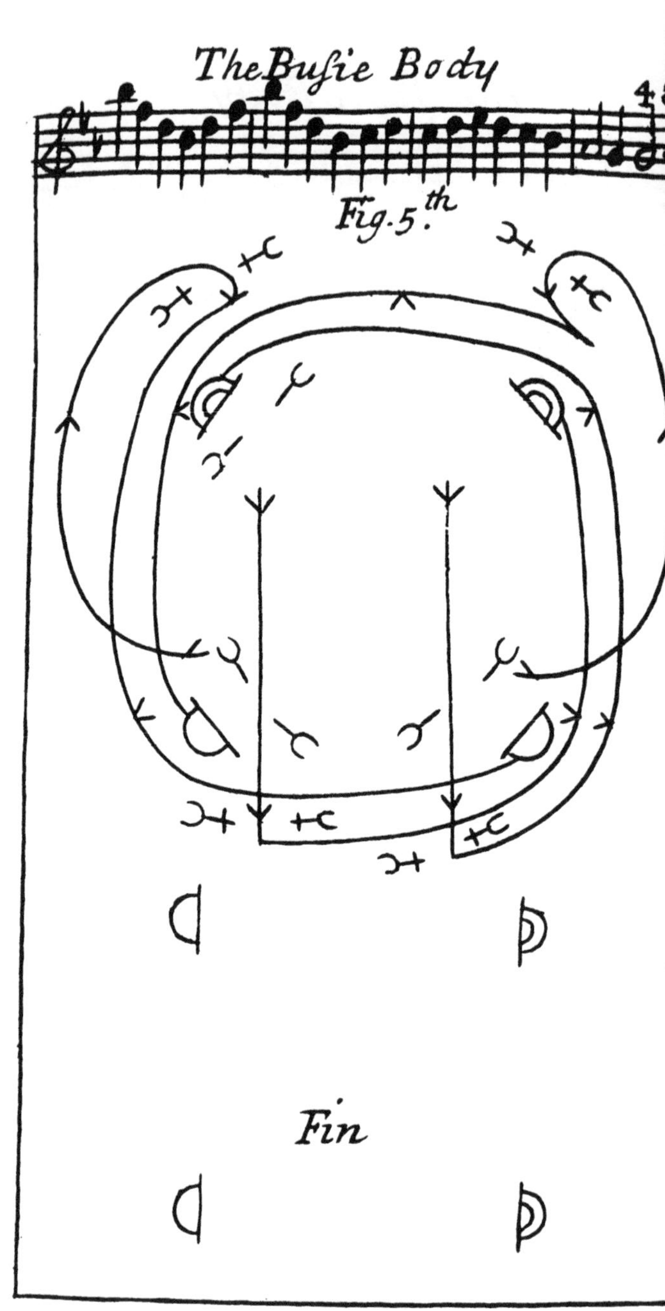
The Busie Body
Fig. 5th
Fin

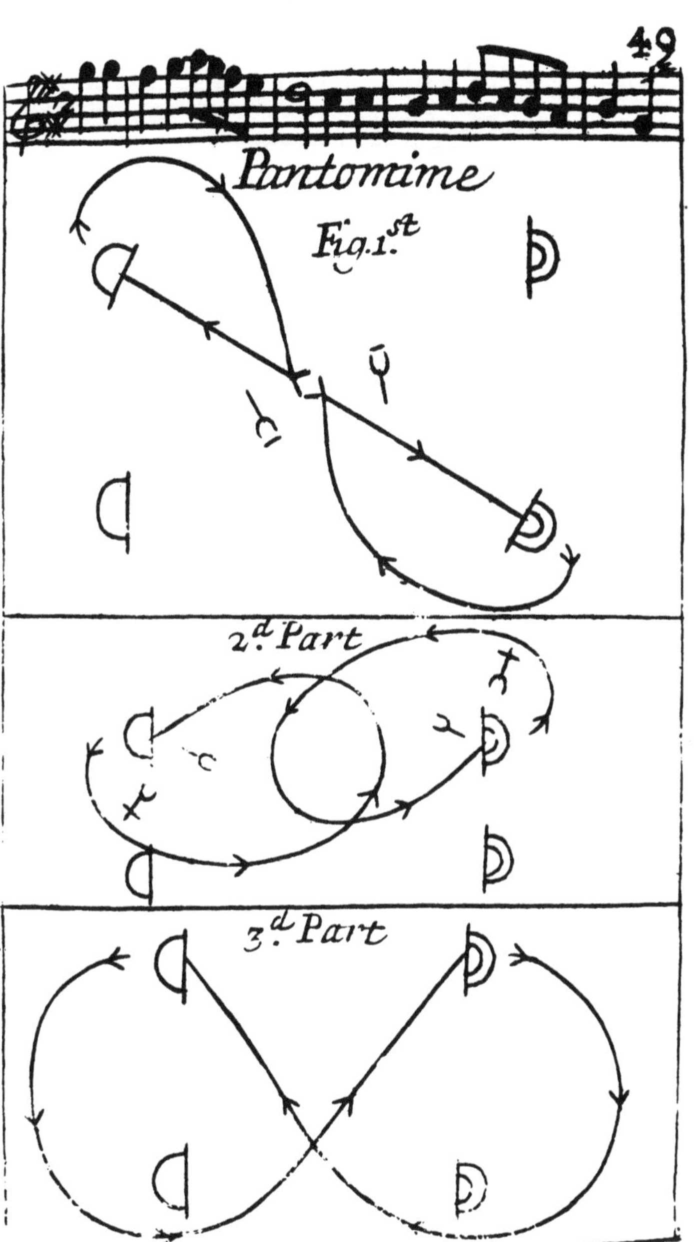
Pantomime
Fig.1.st
2.d Part
3.d Part

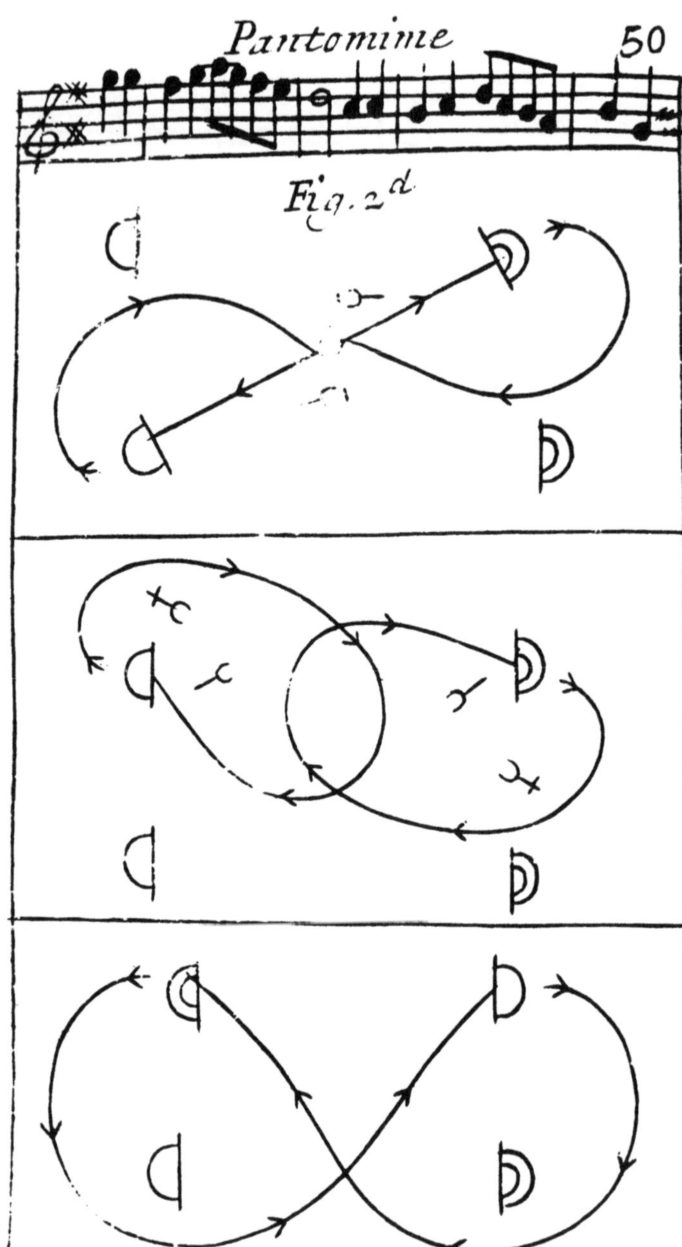
Pantomime
Fig. 2d

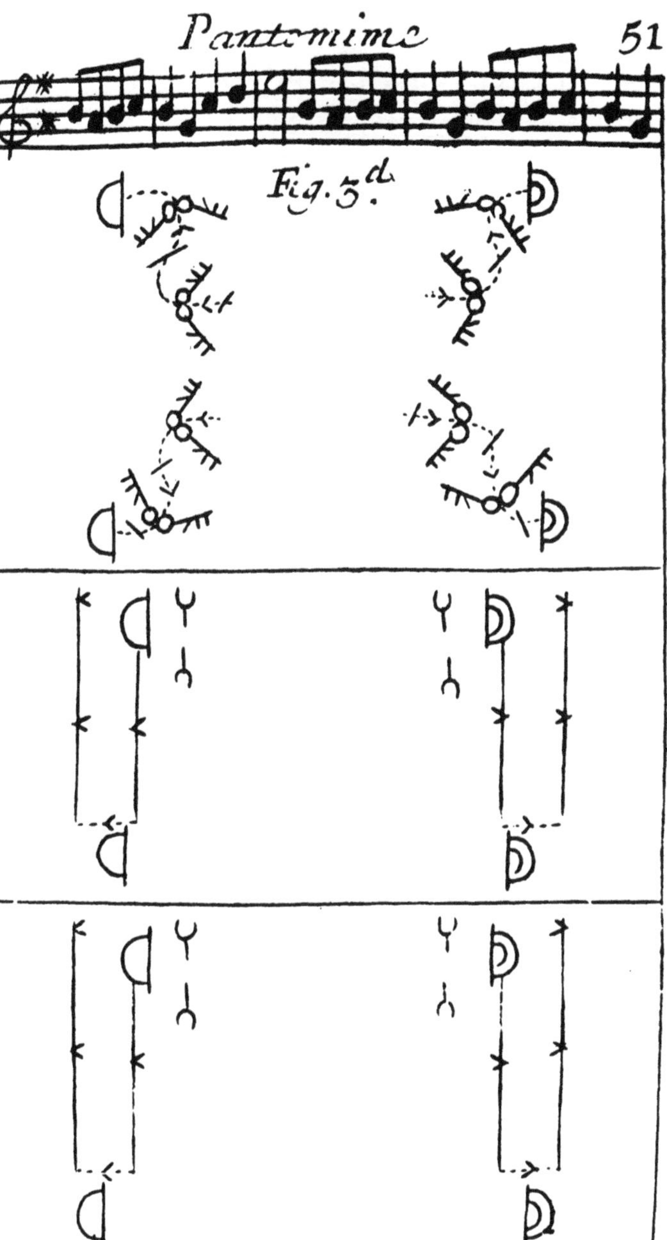
Fig. 3.d

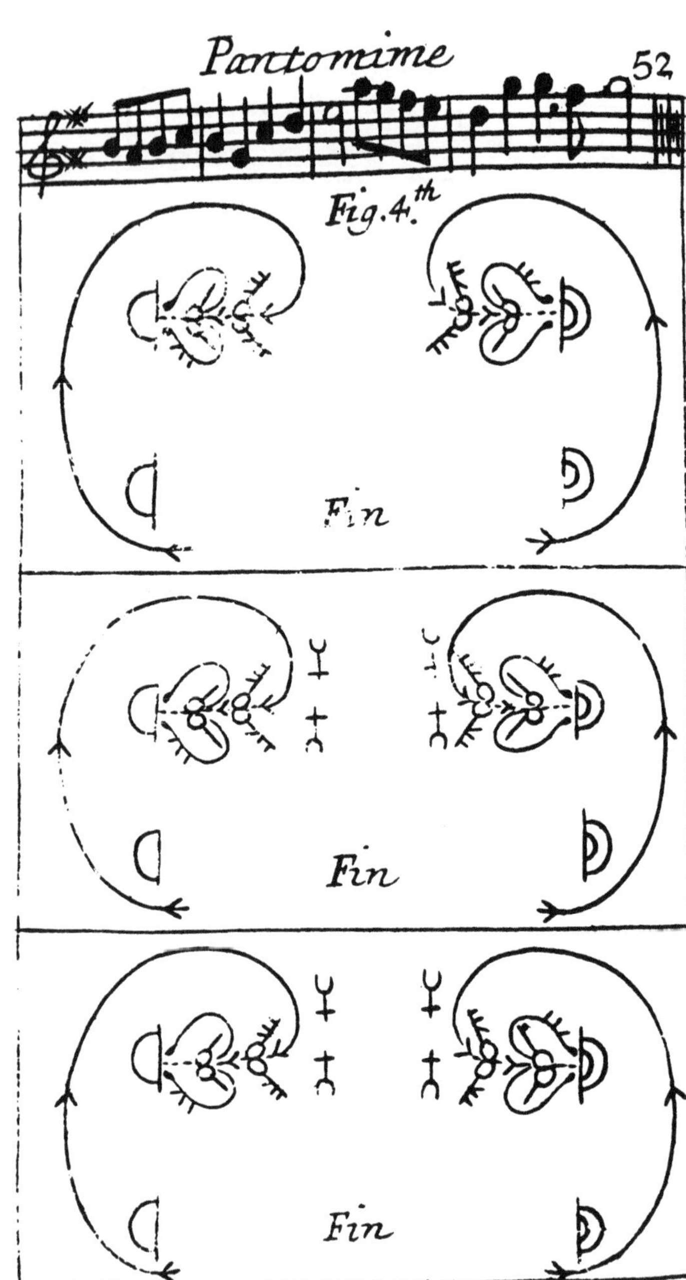
Pantomime
52
Fig. 4.th
Fin
Fin
Fin

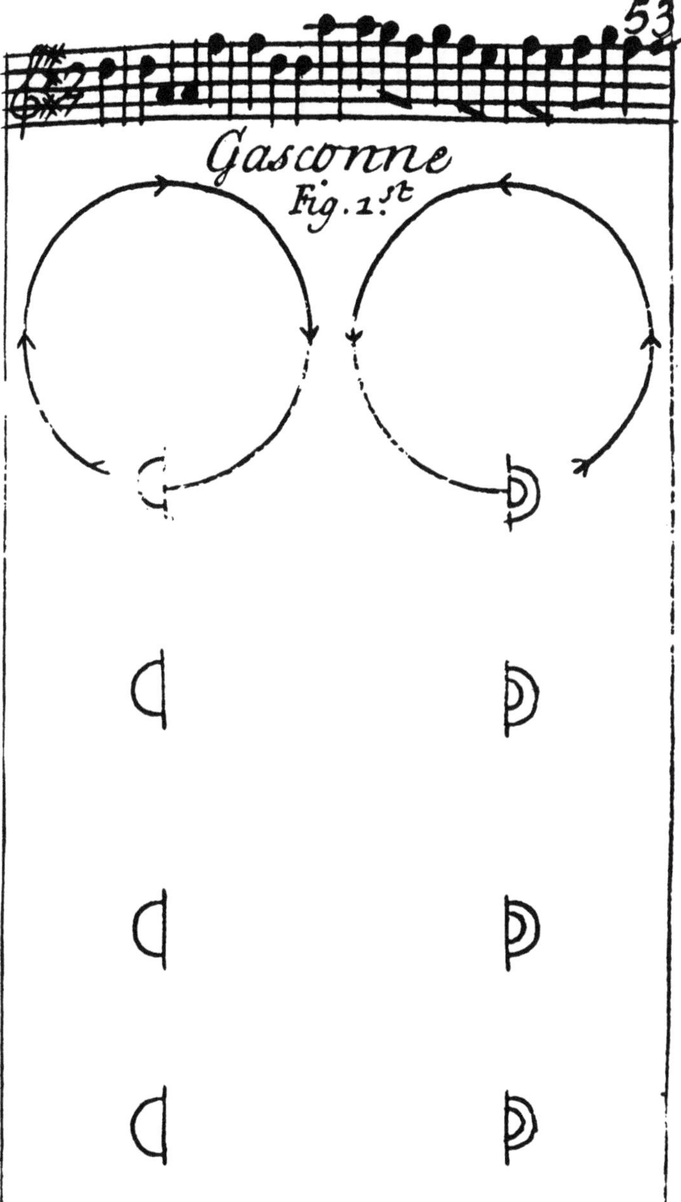
Gasconne
Fig. 1.st

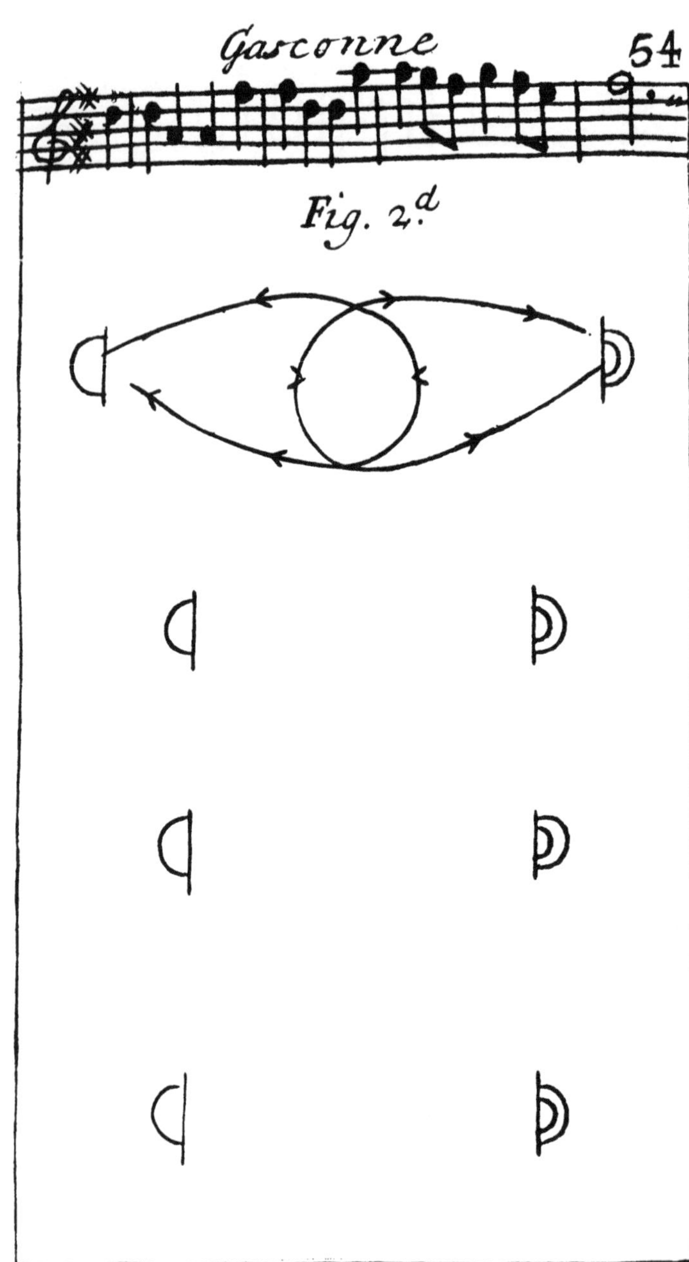
Gasconne
Fig. 2.d

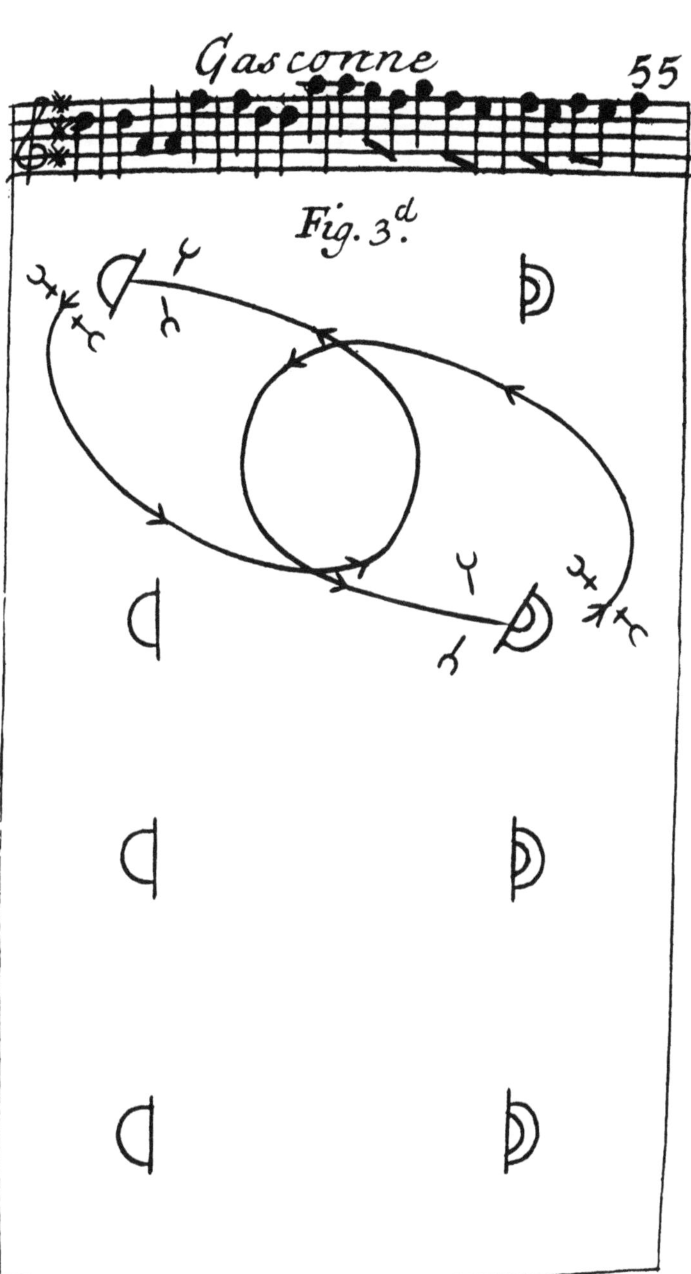
Gasconne
Fig. 3d.

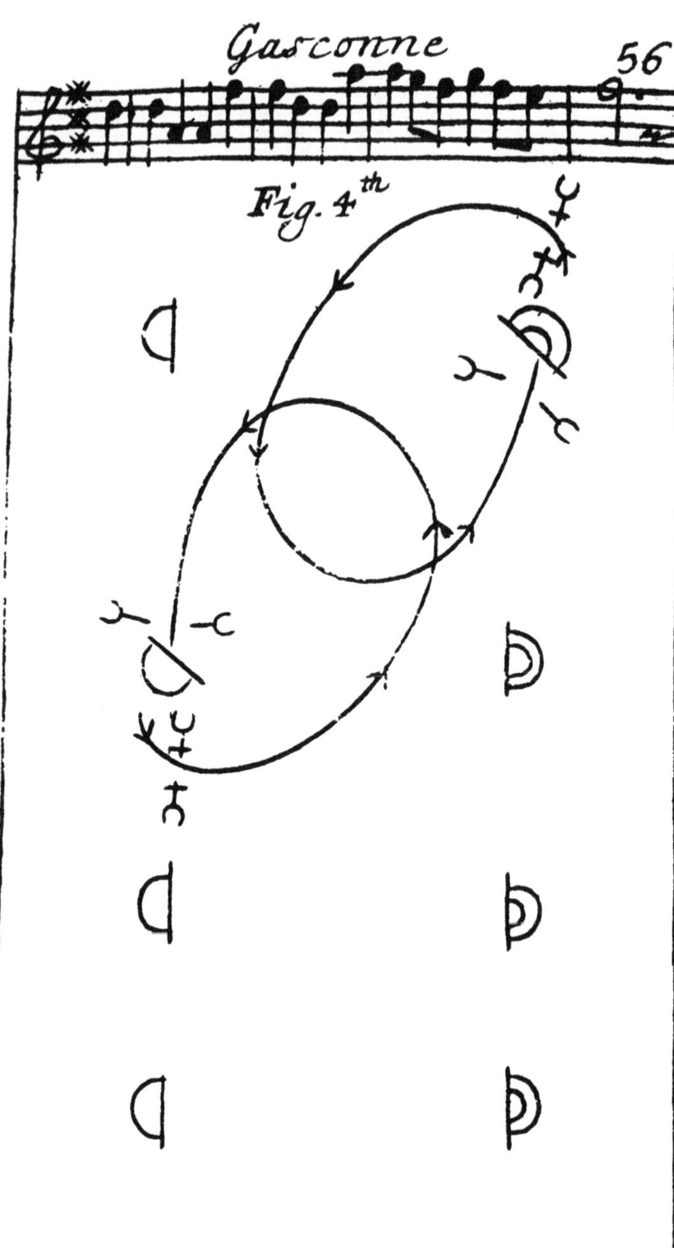
Gasconne
Fig. 4th

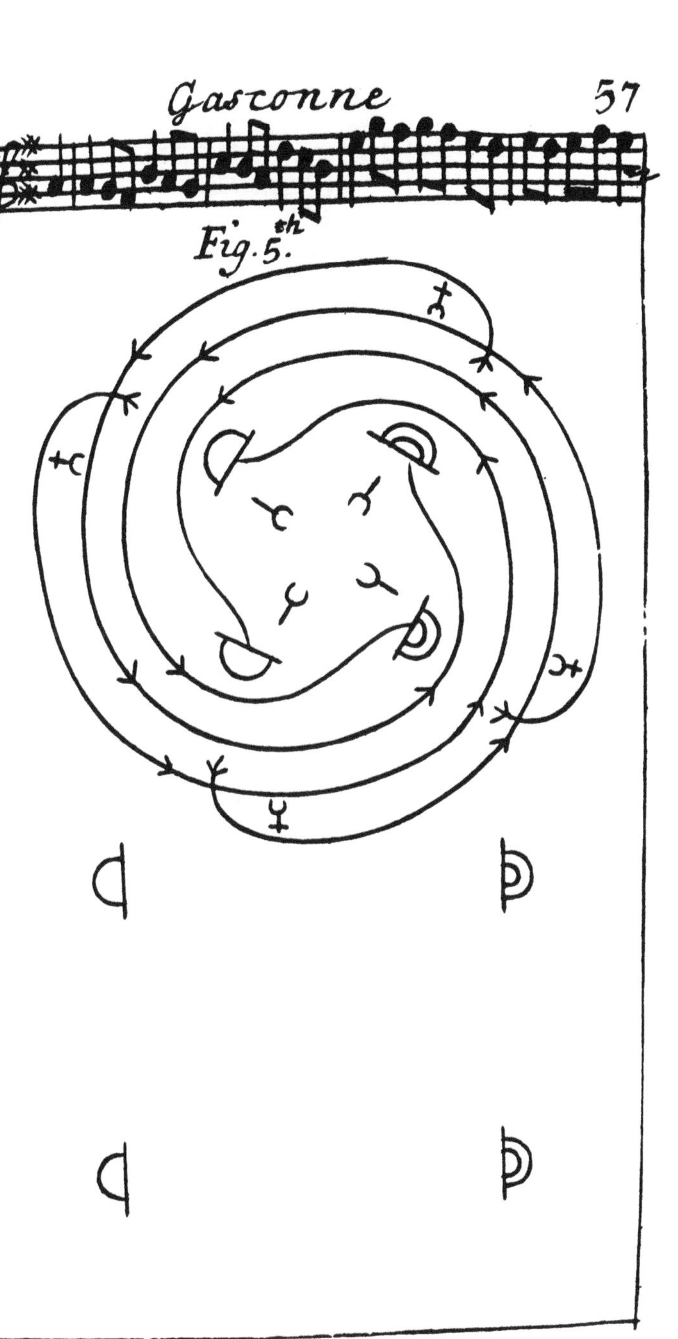
Gasconne
Fig. 5th

Gasconne

Fig. 6th

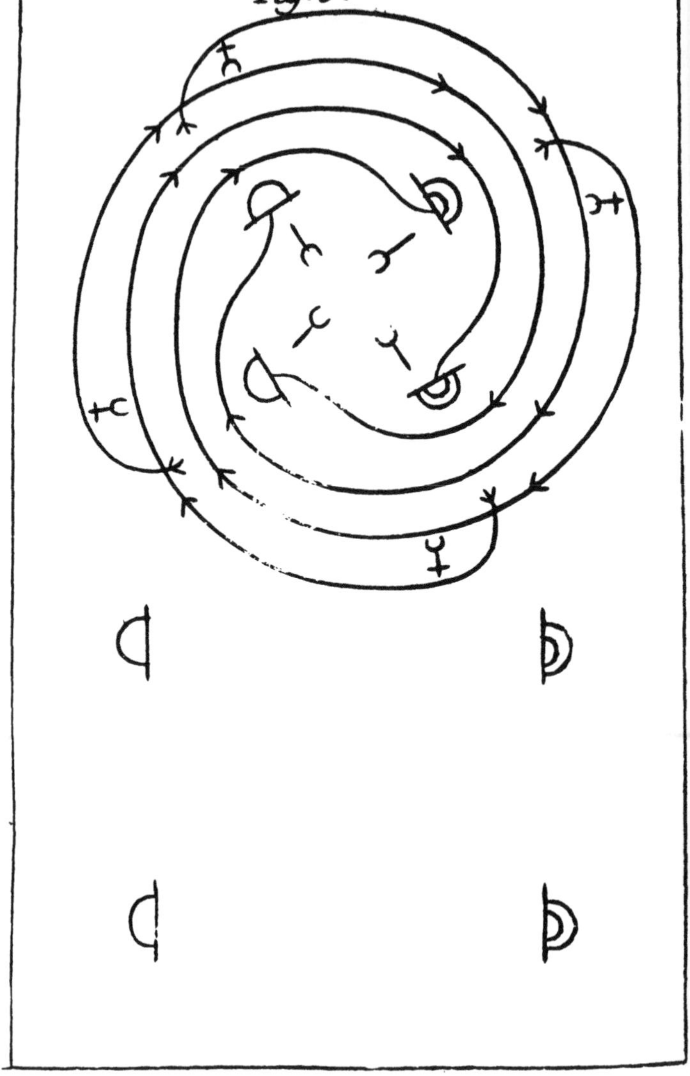

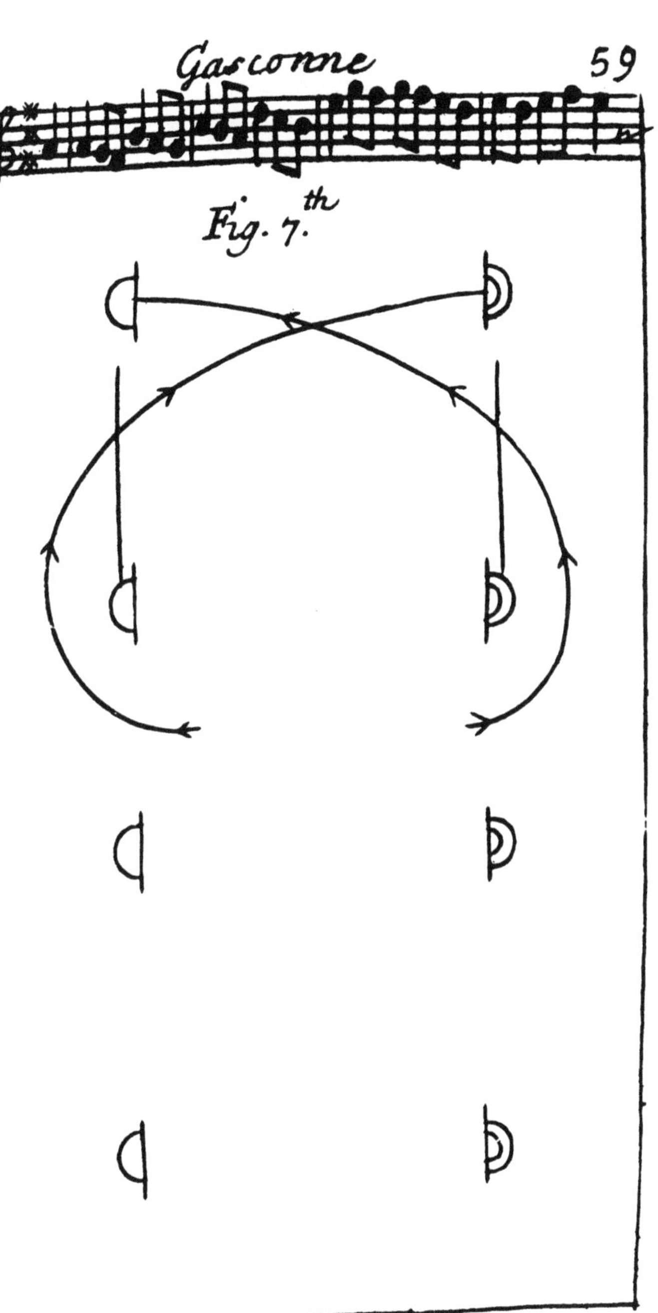

Fig. 7th.

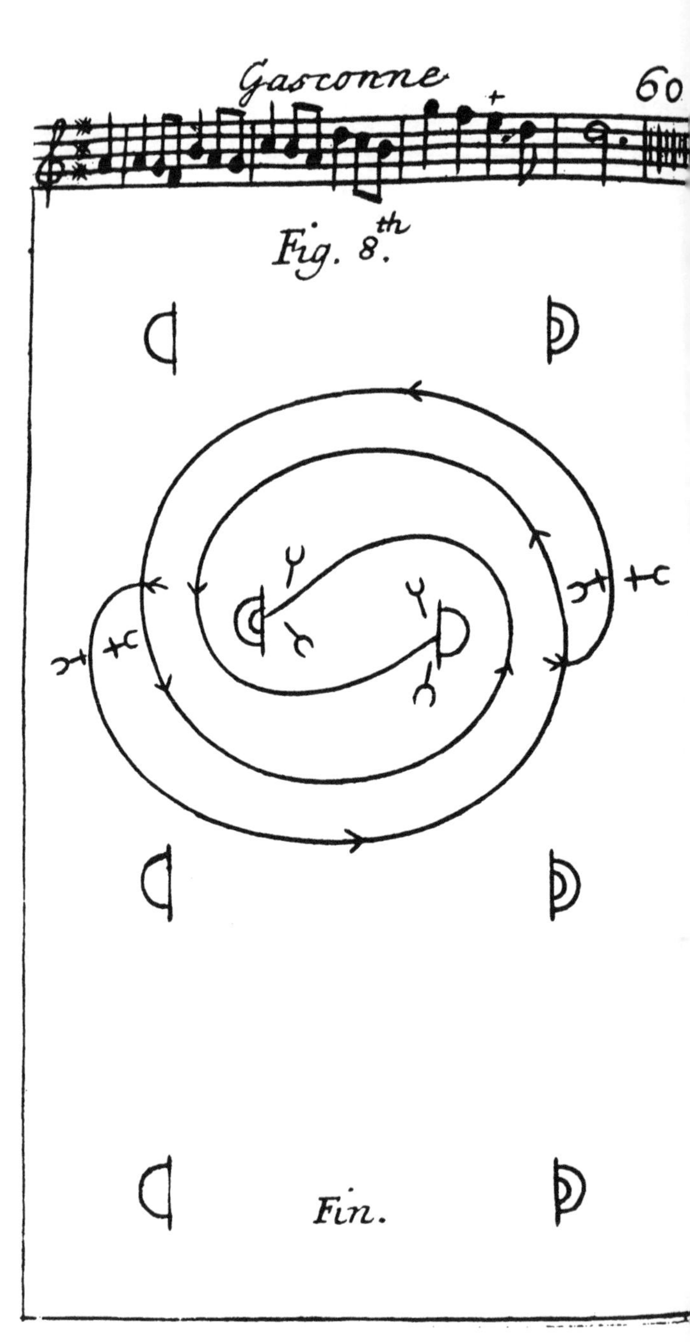
Gasconne
Fig. 8.th
Fin.

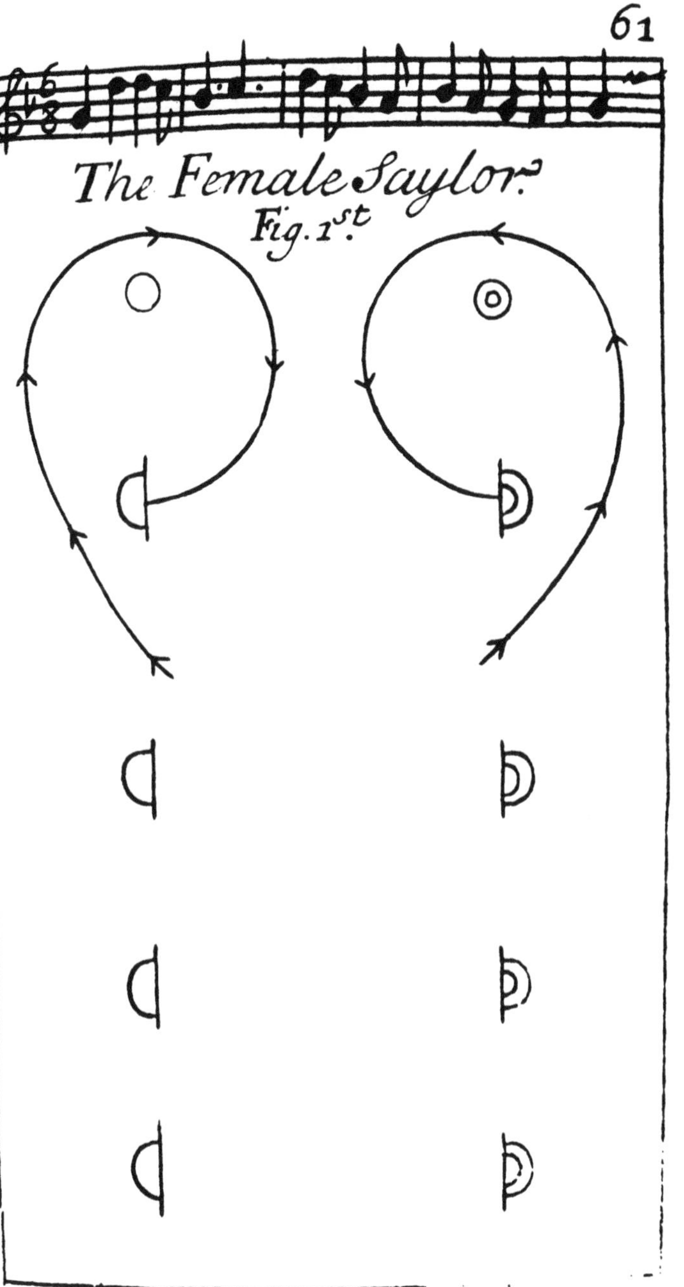
The Female Saylor.
Fig. 1st.

The Female Saylor

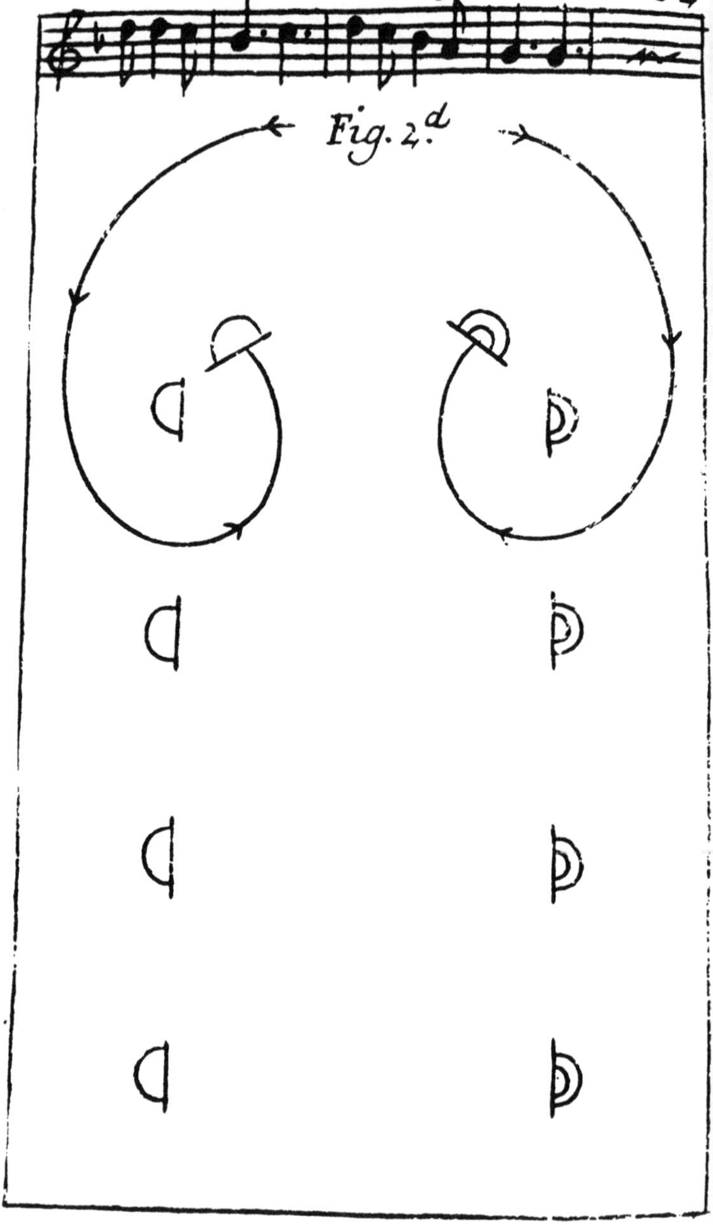

Fig. 2.d

The Female Saylor

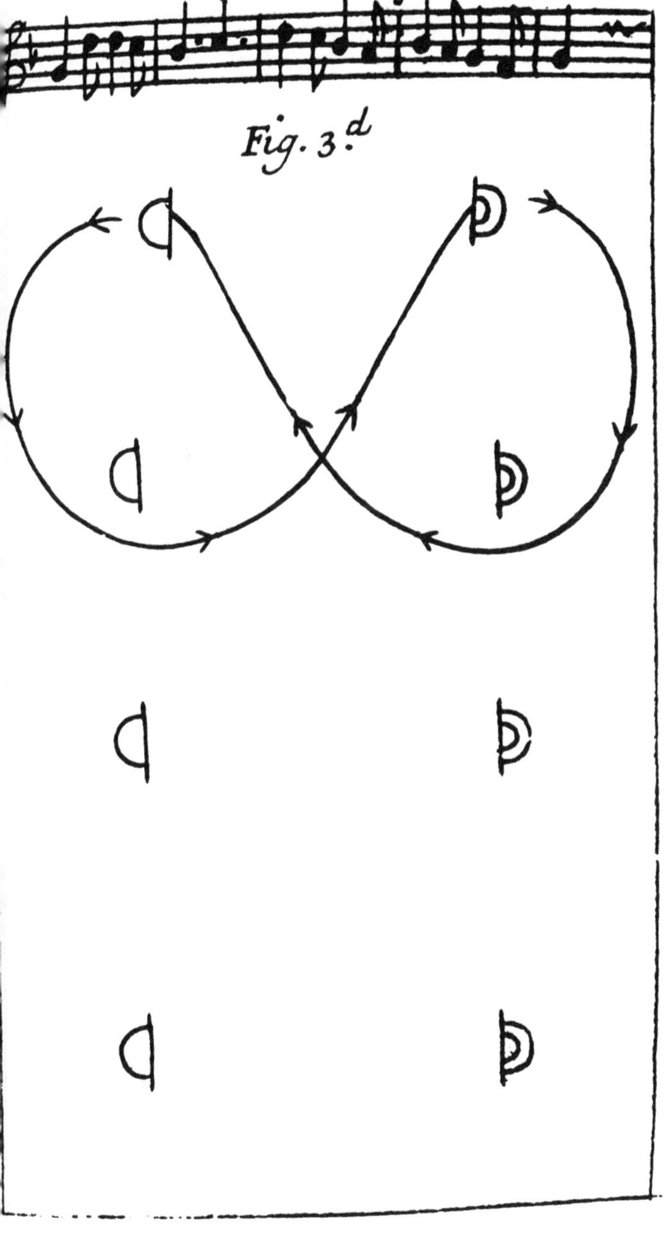

Fig. 3.d

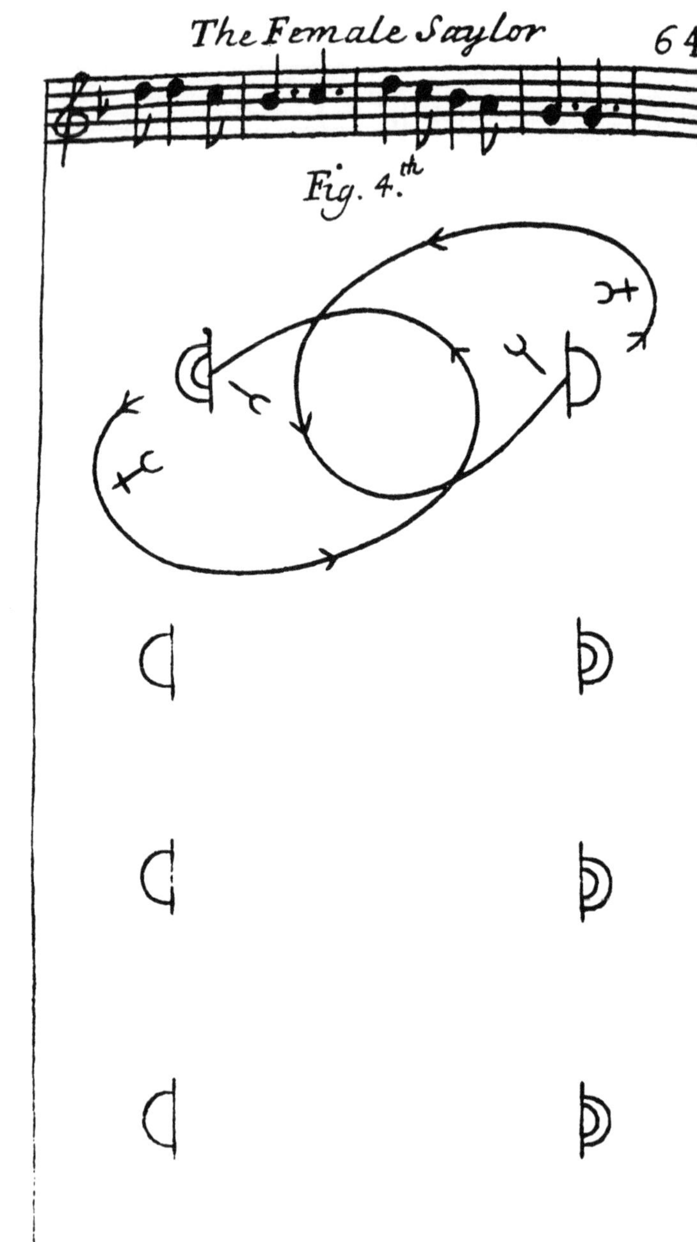
The Female Saylor
Fig. 4.th

Fig. 5.th

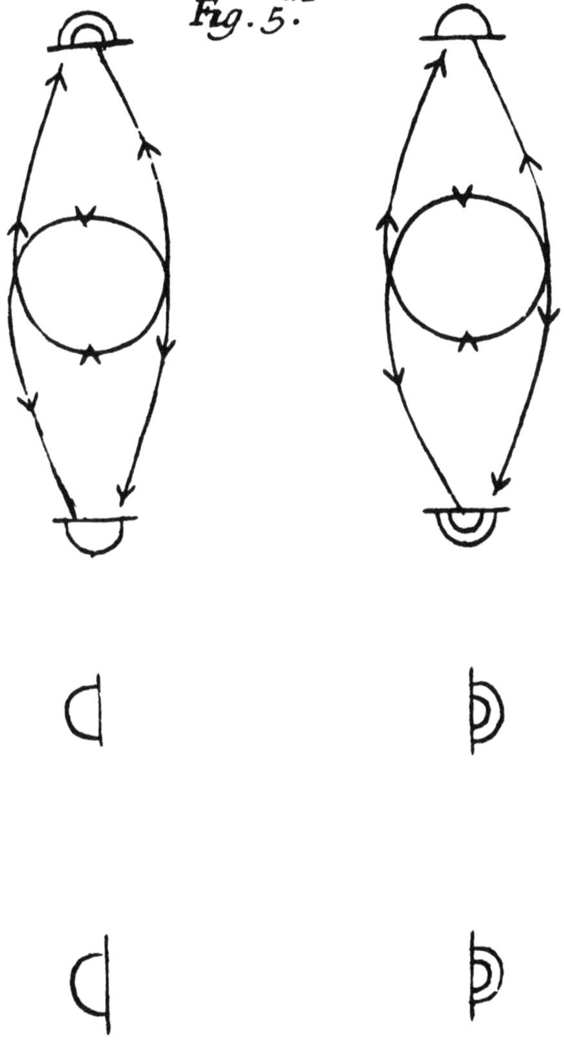

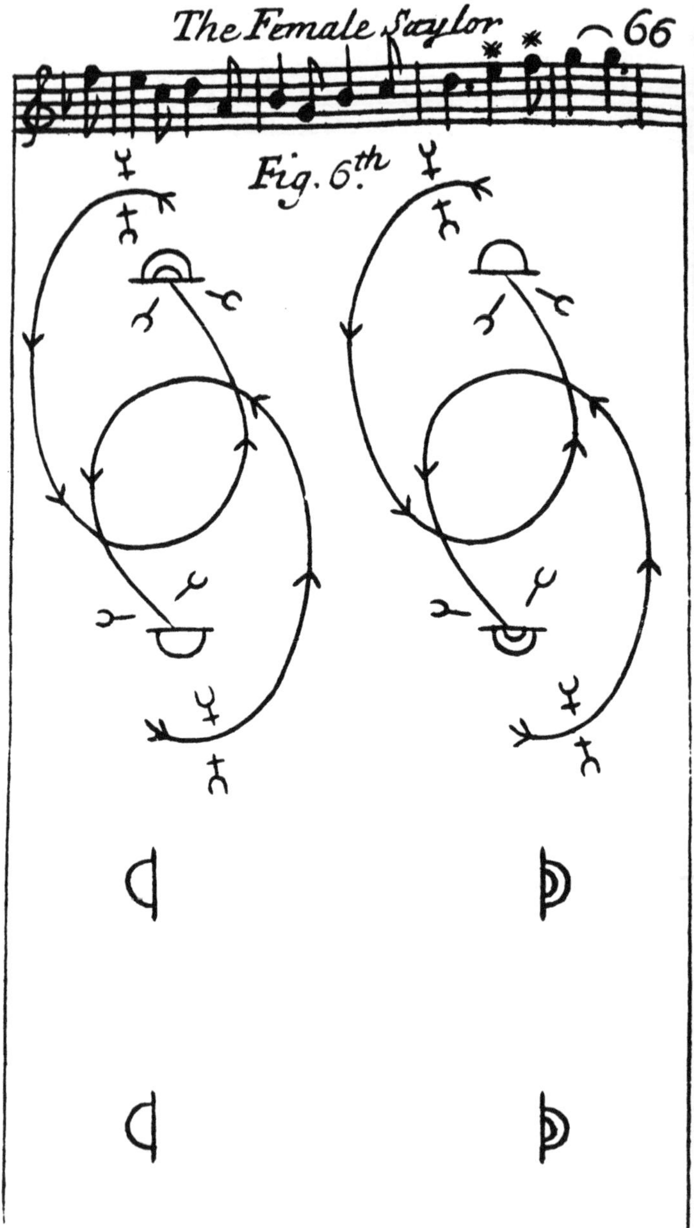

The Female Saylor

Fig. 6th

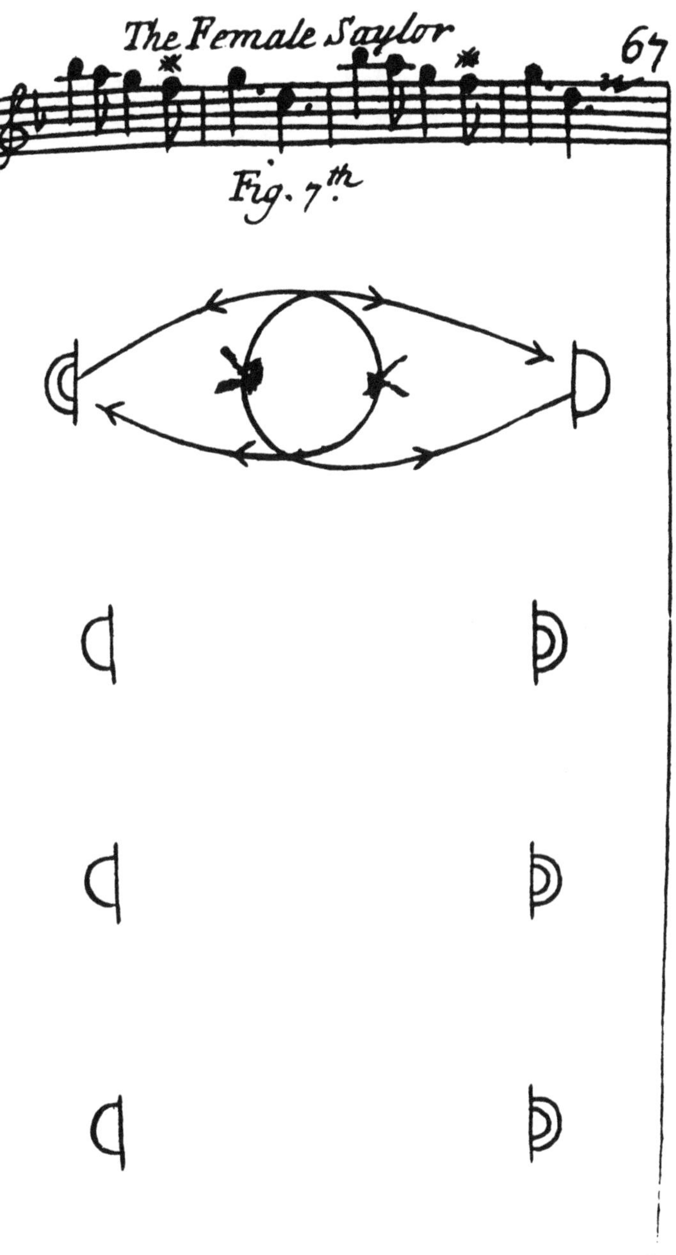
The Female Saylor
Fig. 7th.

The Female Saylor

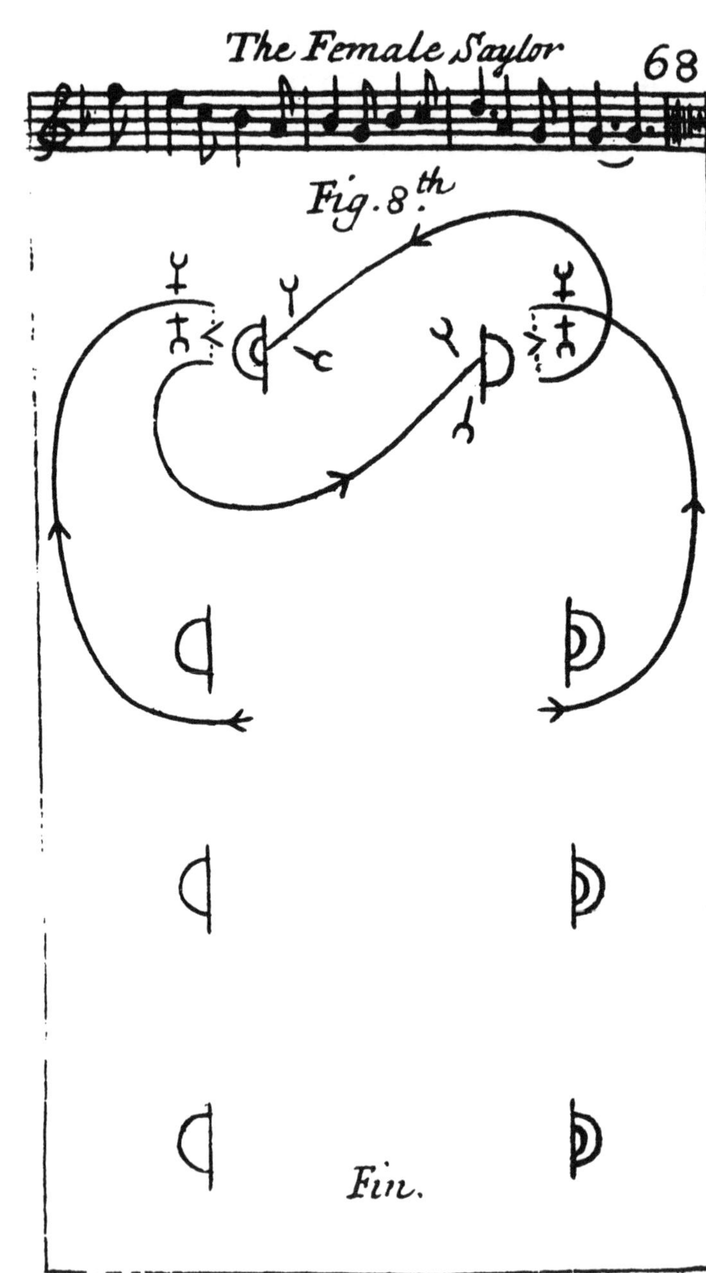

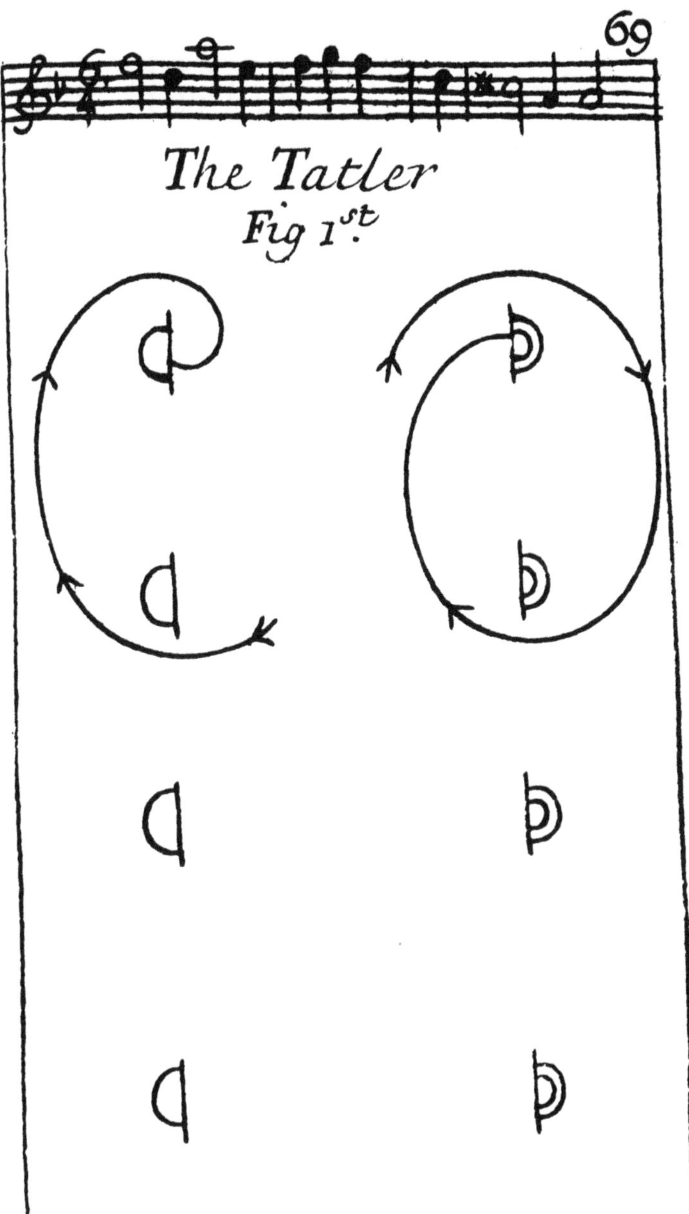
The Tatler
Fig 1st.

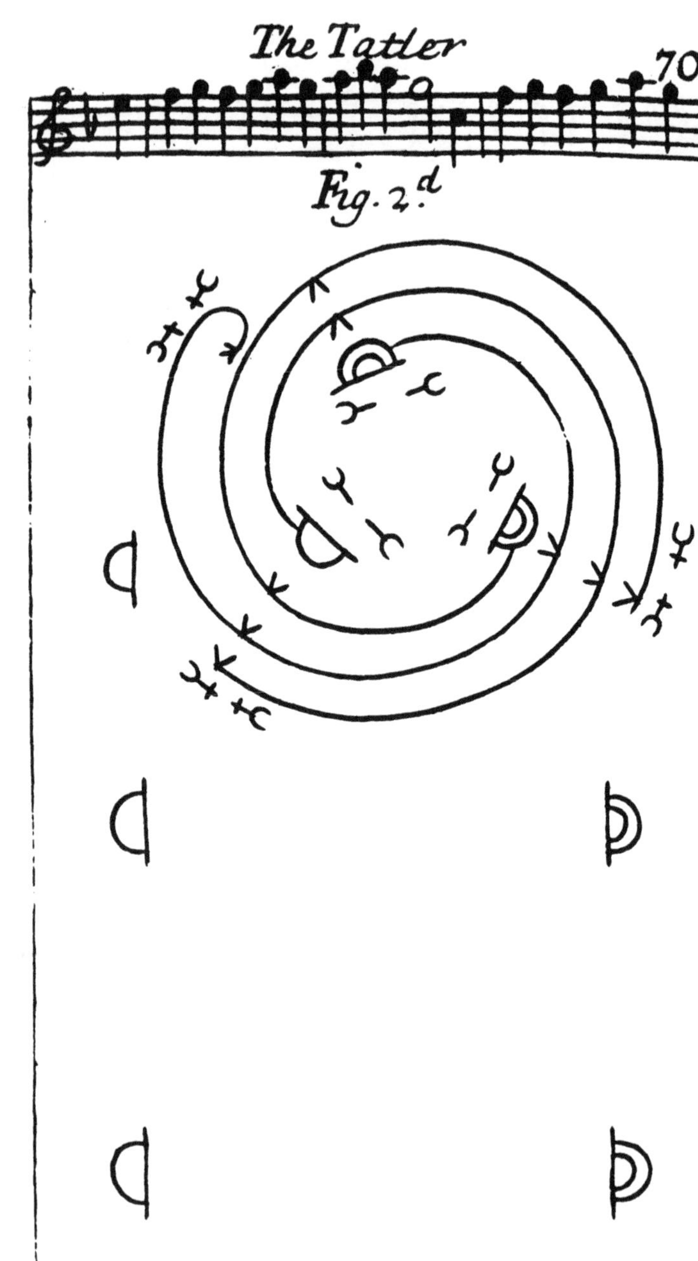

The Tatler
70
Fig. 2.d

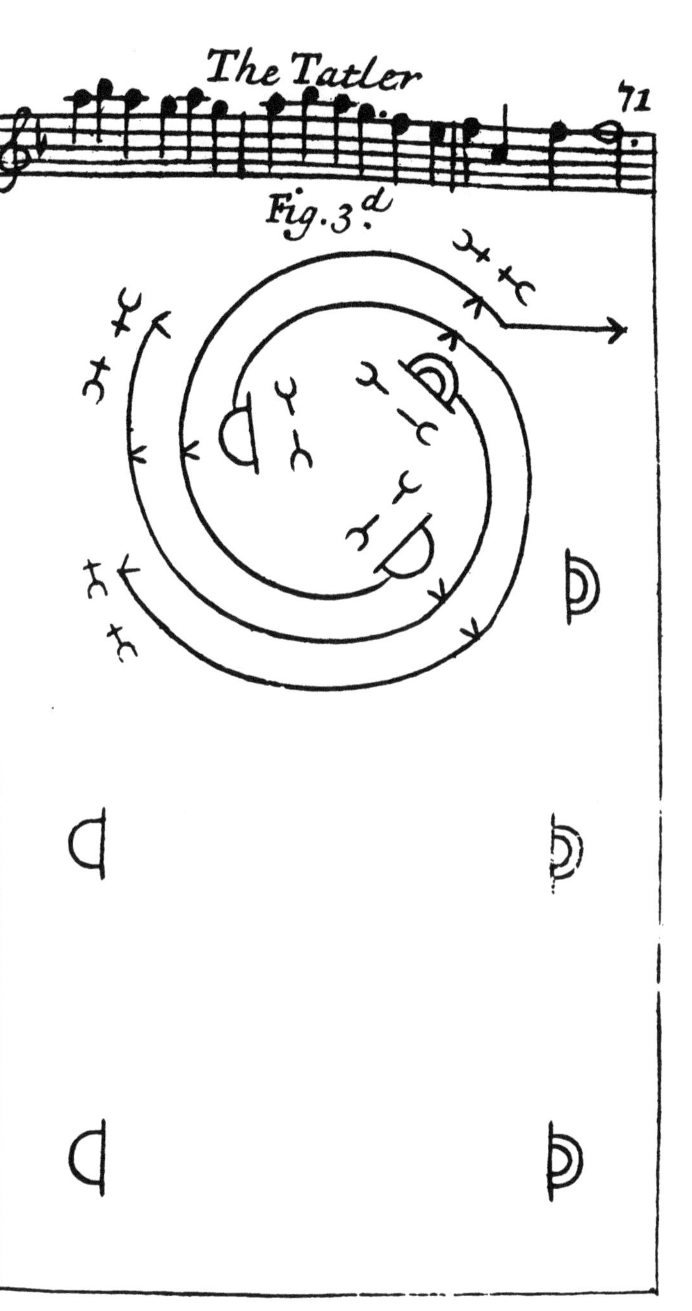

Fig. 3d

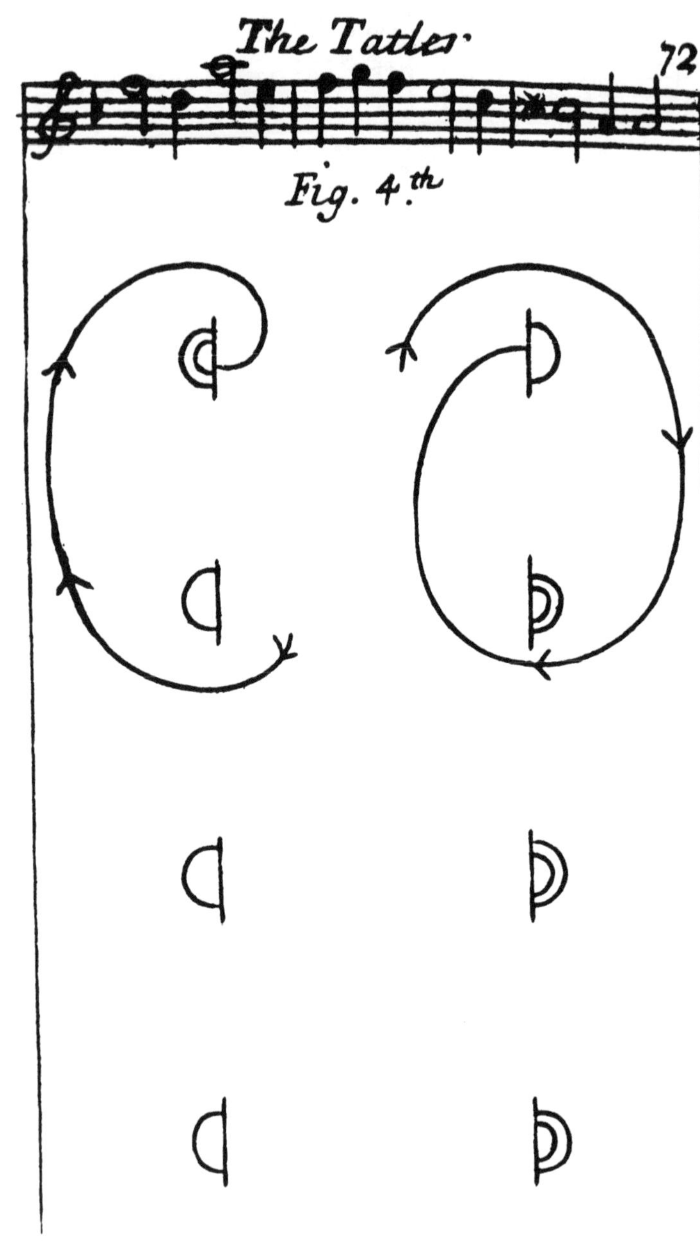
Fig. 4.th

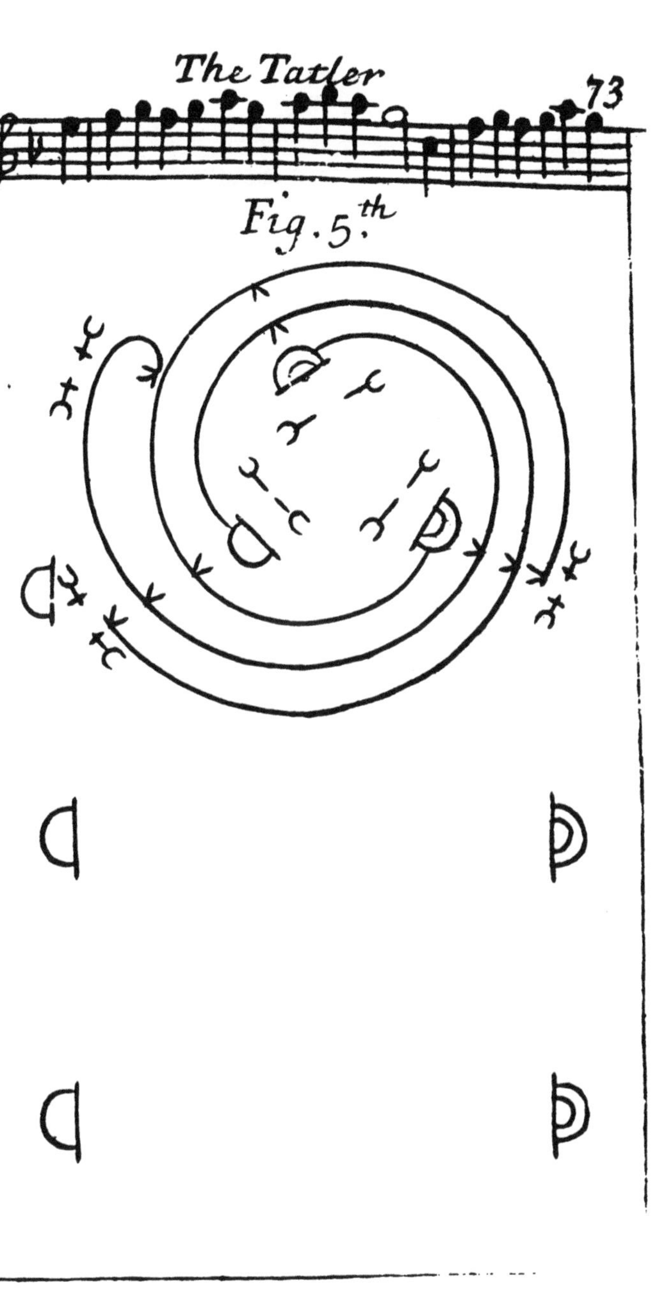
The Tatler
73
Fig. 5.th

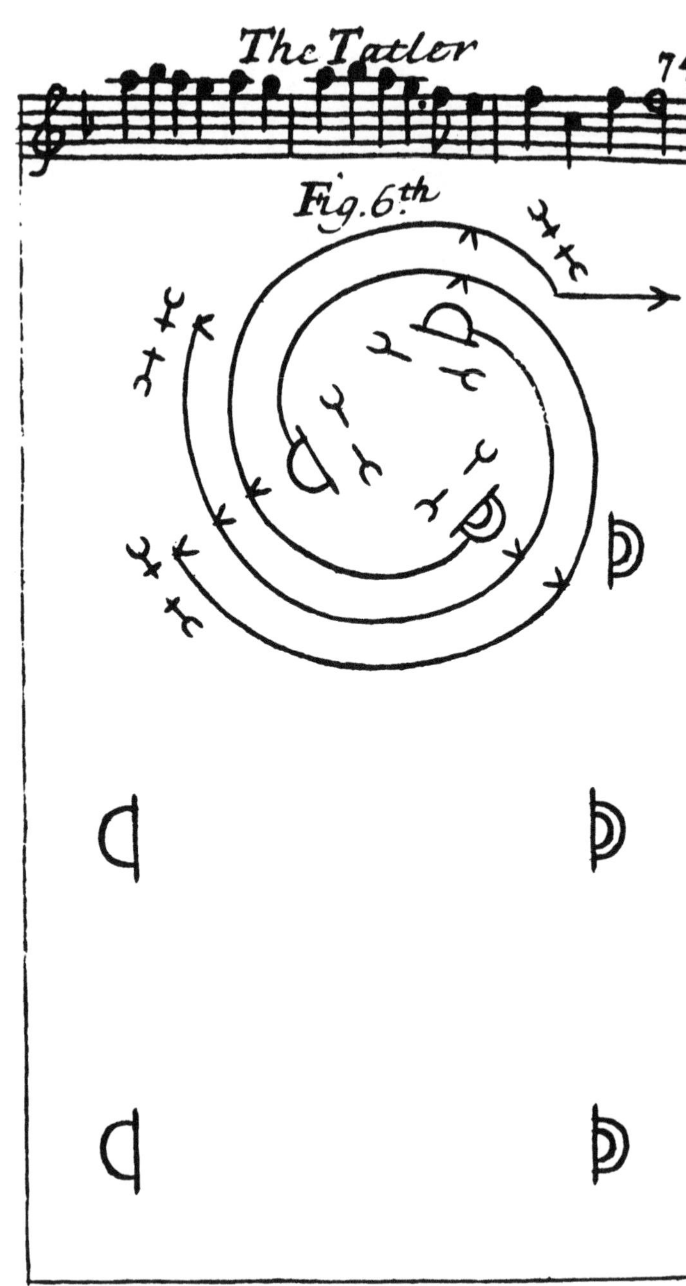
The Tatler
74
Fig. 6th

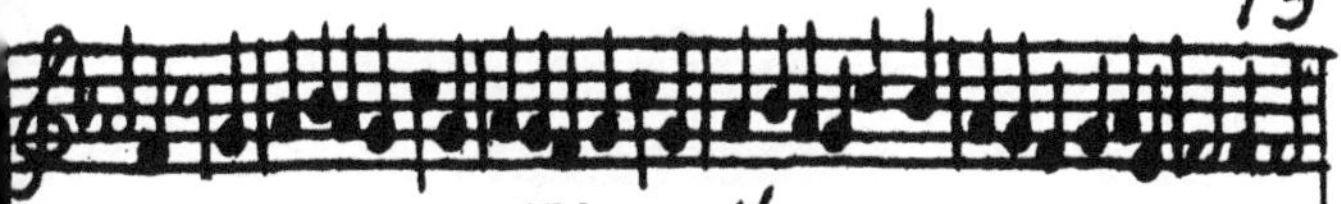

Fig. 7th

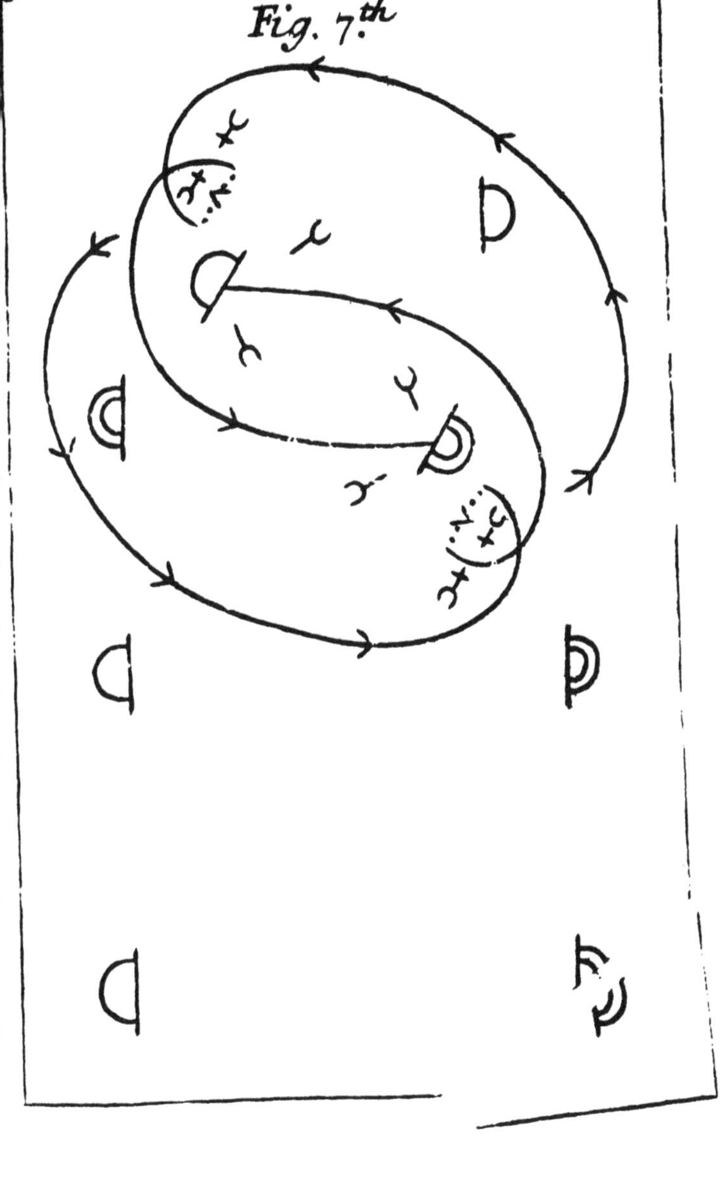

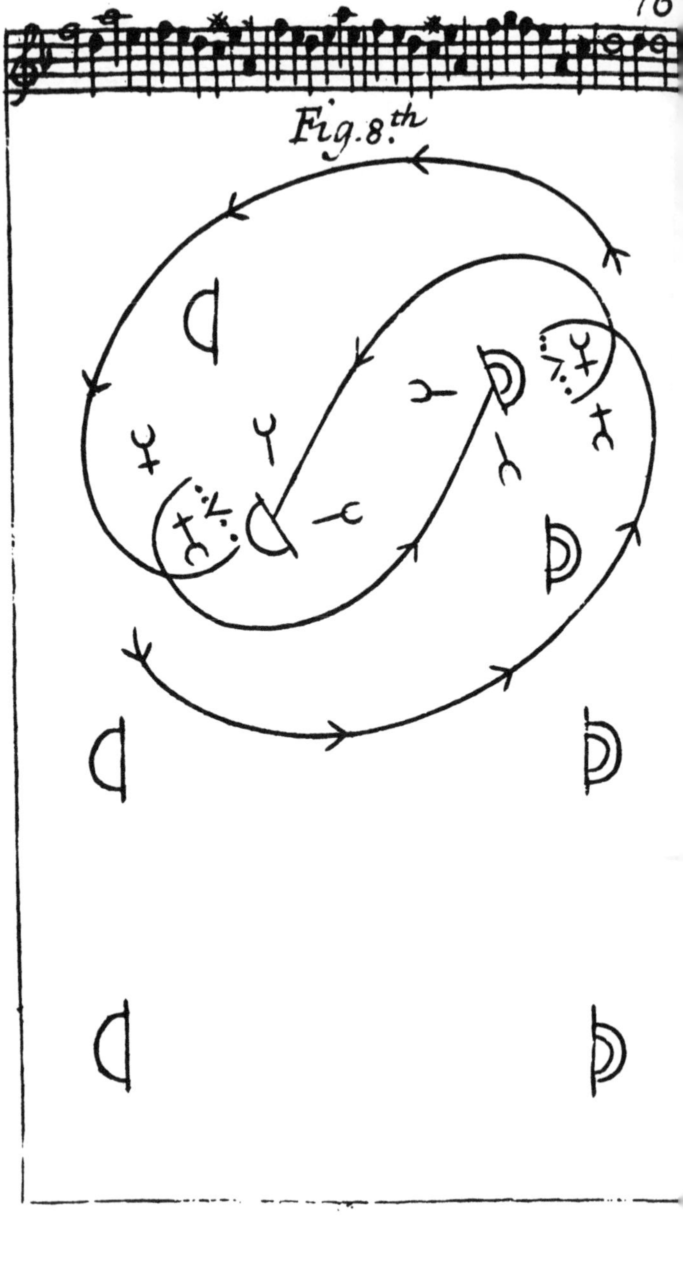

Fig. 8.th

The Tatler

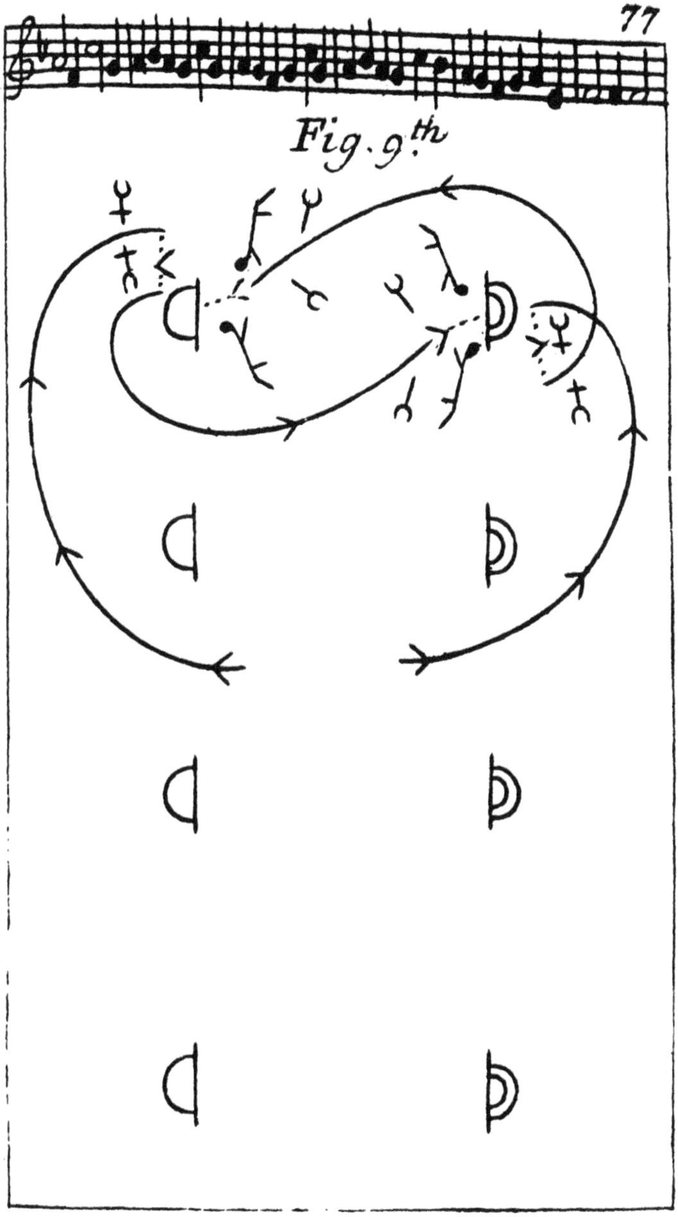

Fig. 9th

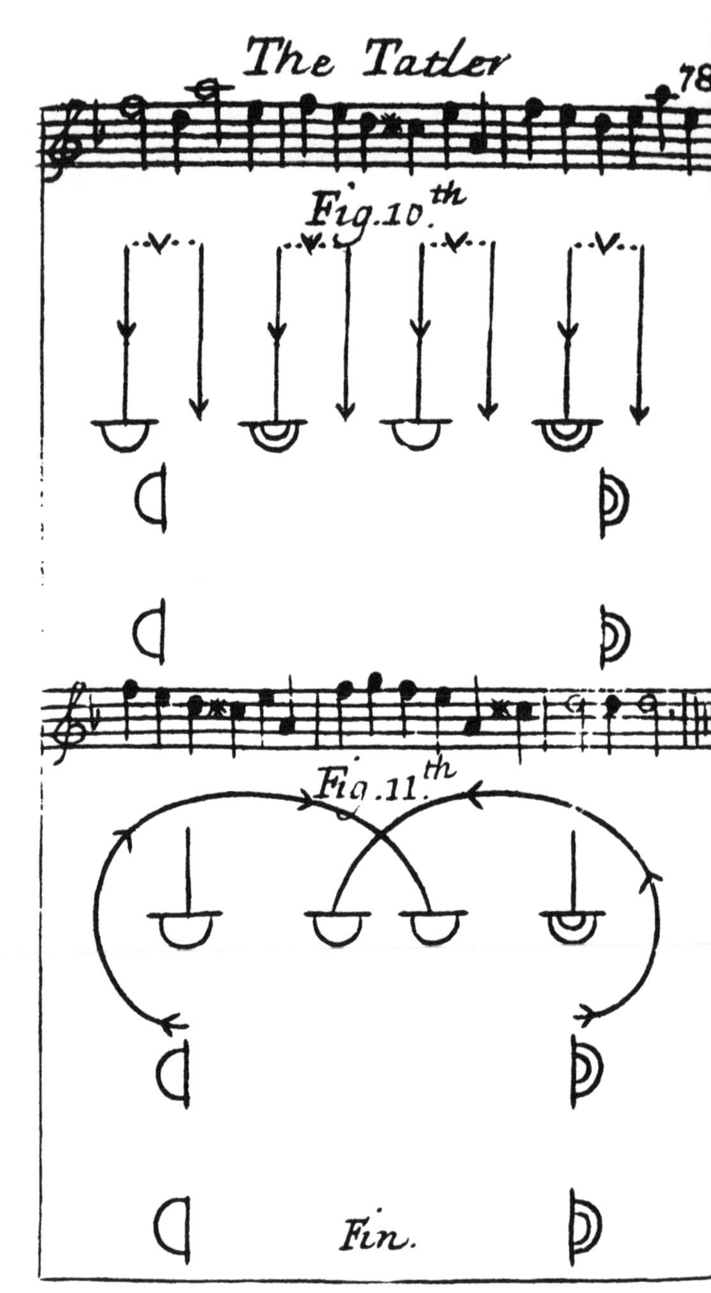
The Tatler
78
Fig.10.th
Fig.11.th
Fin.

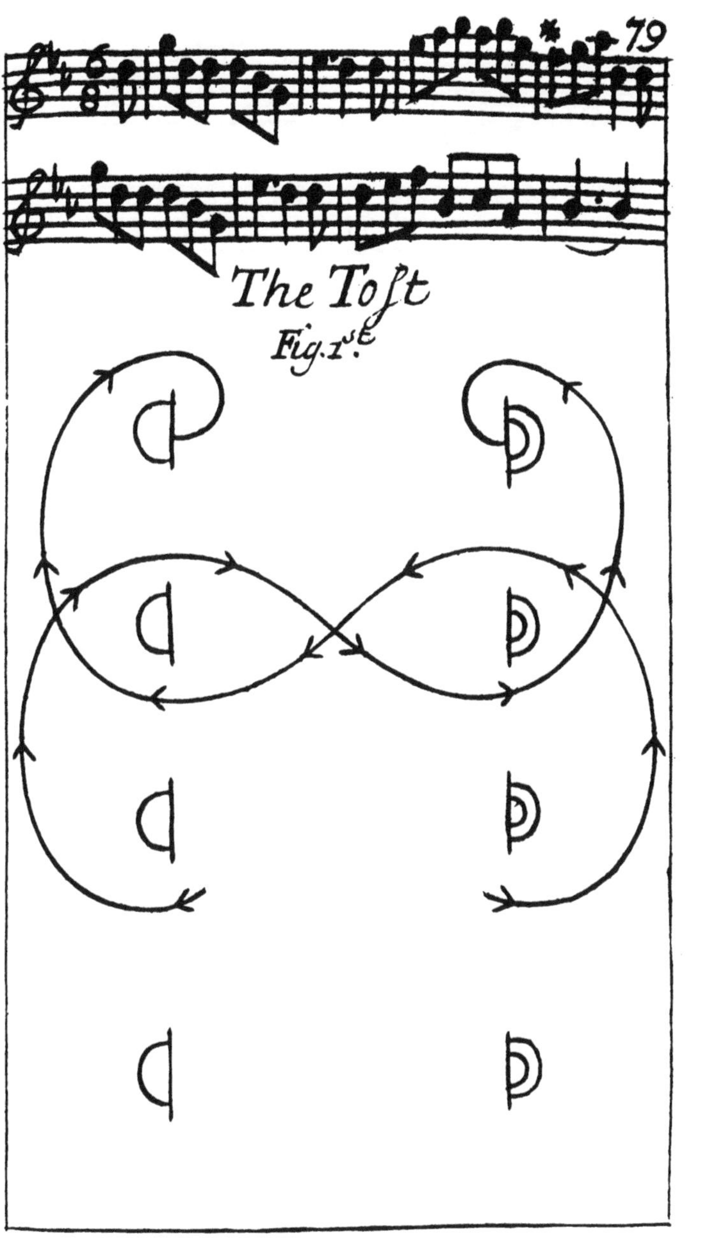
The Tost
Fig. 1st

The Tost

Fig. 2d.

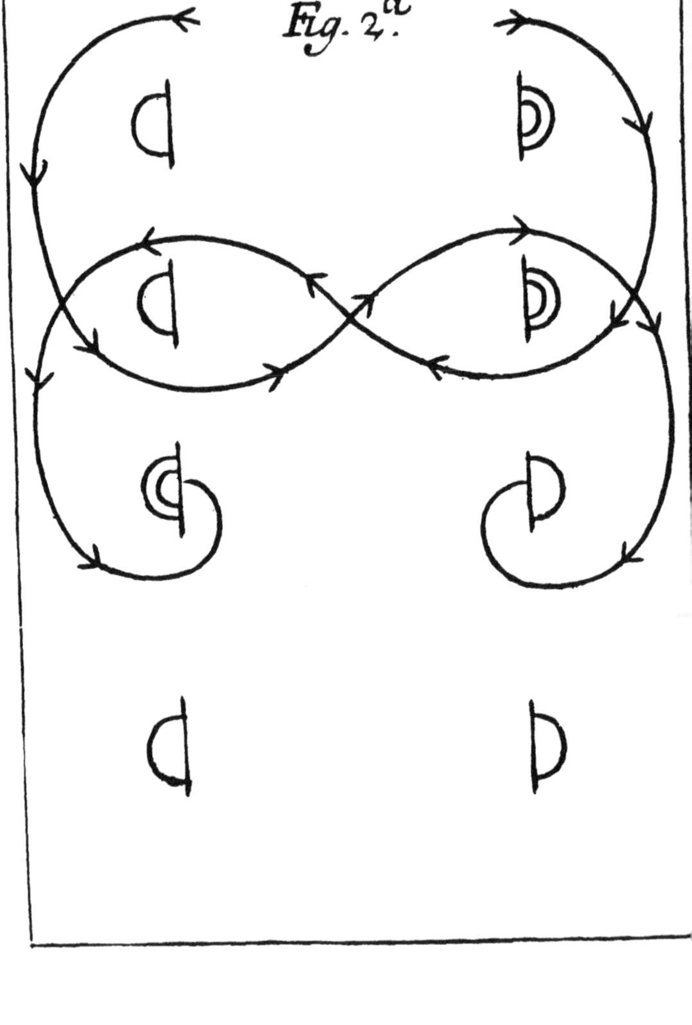

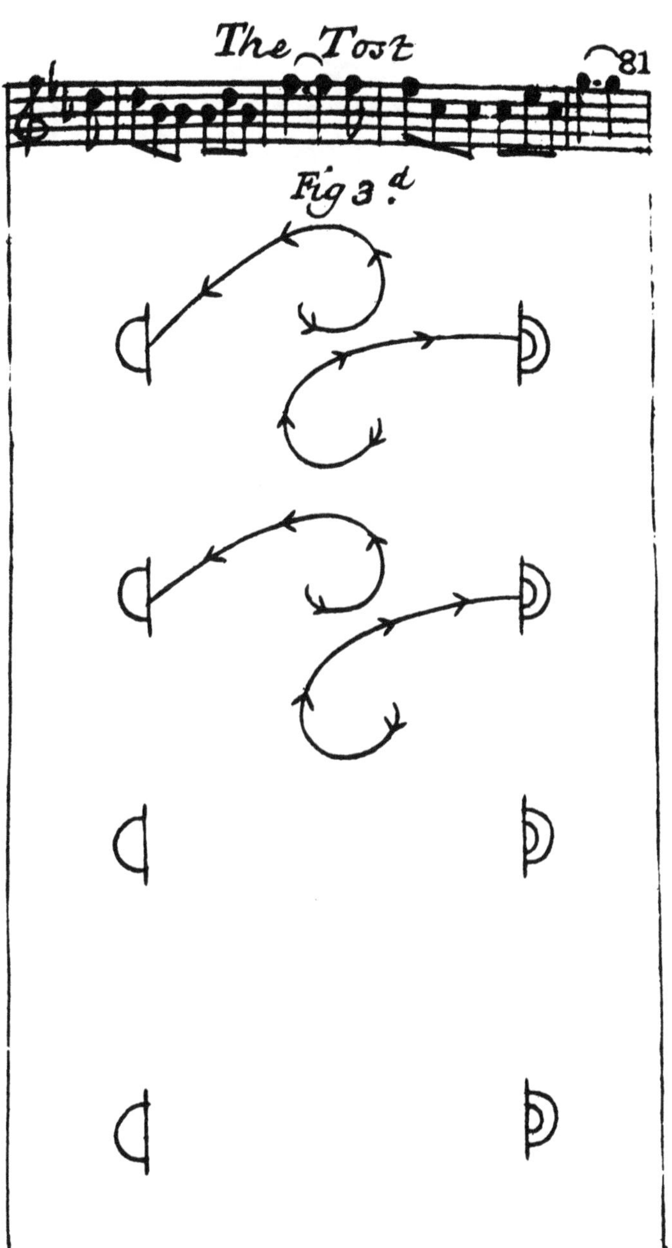
The Tost
81
Fig 3.d

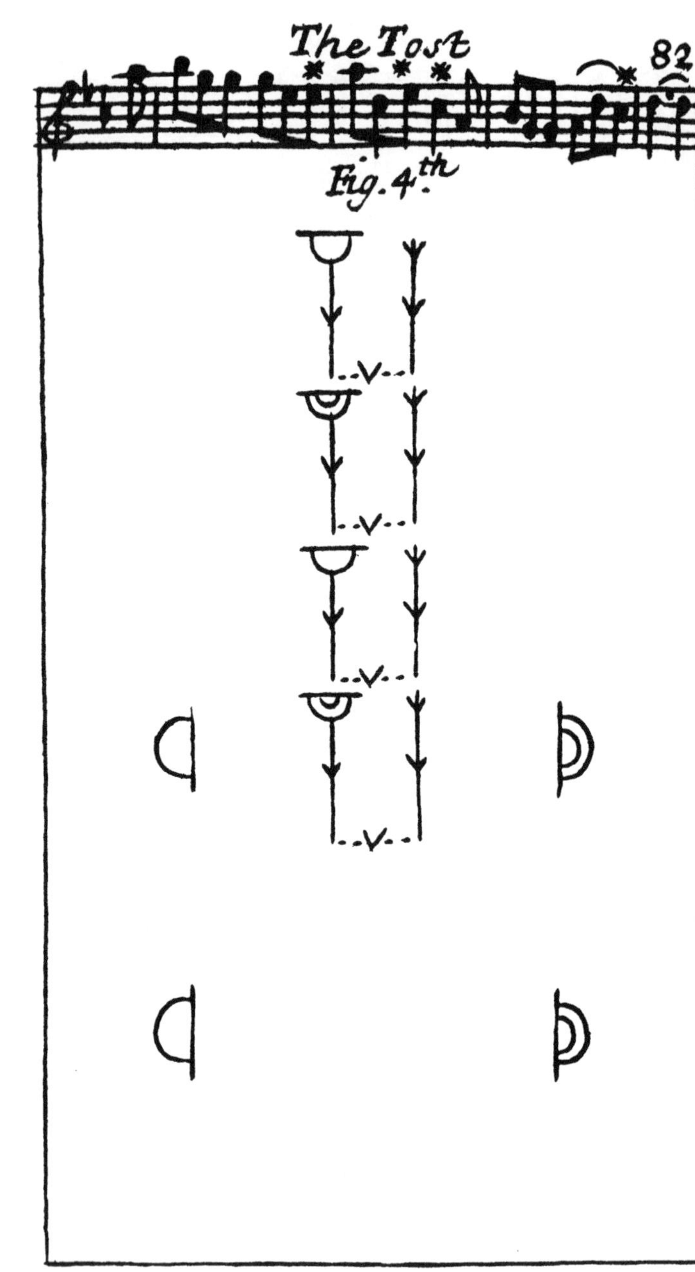
The Tost
82
Fig. 4th

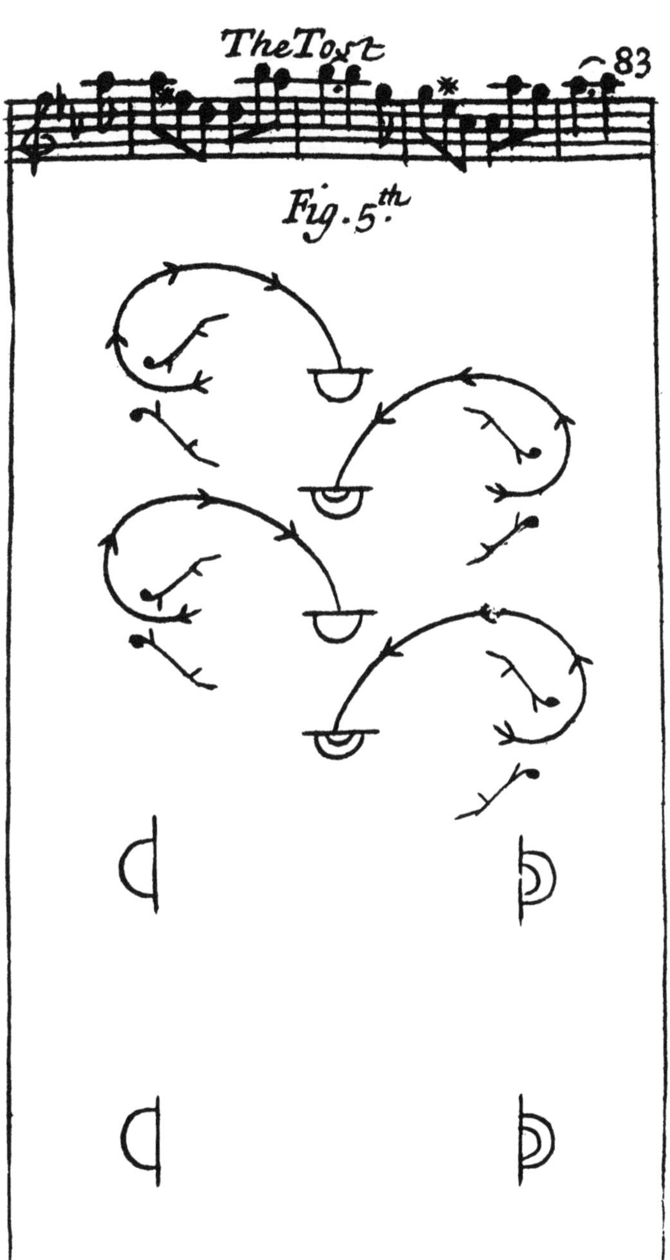
The Tost
Fig. 5th

Fig. 6th

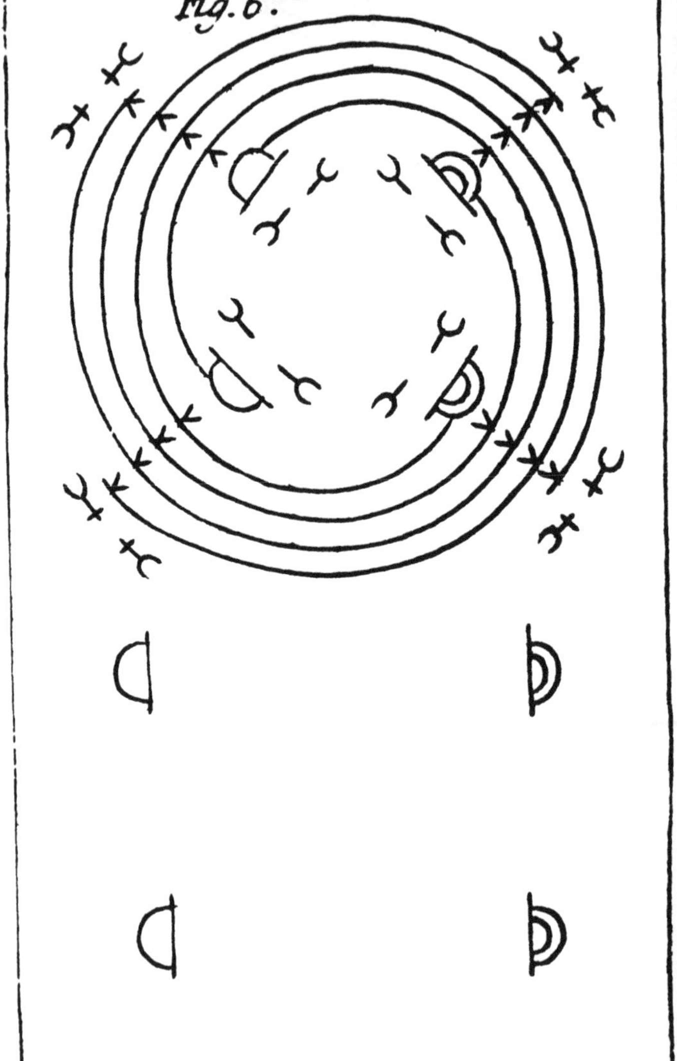

The Tost

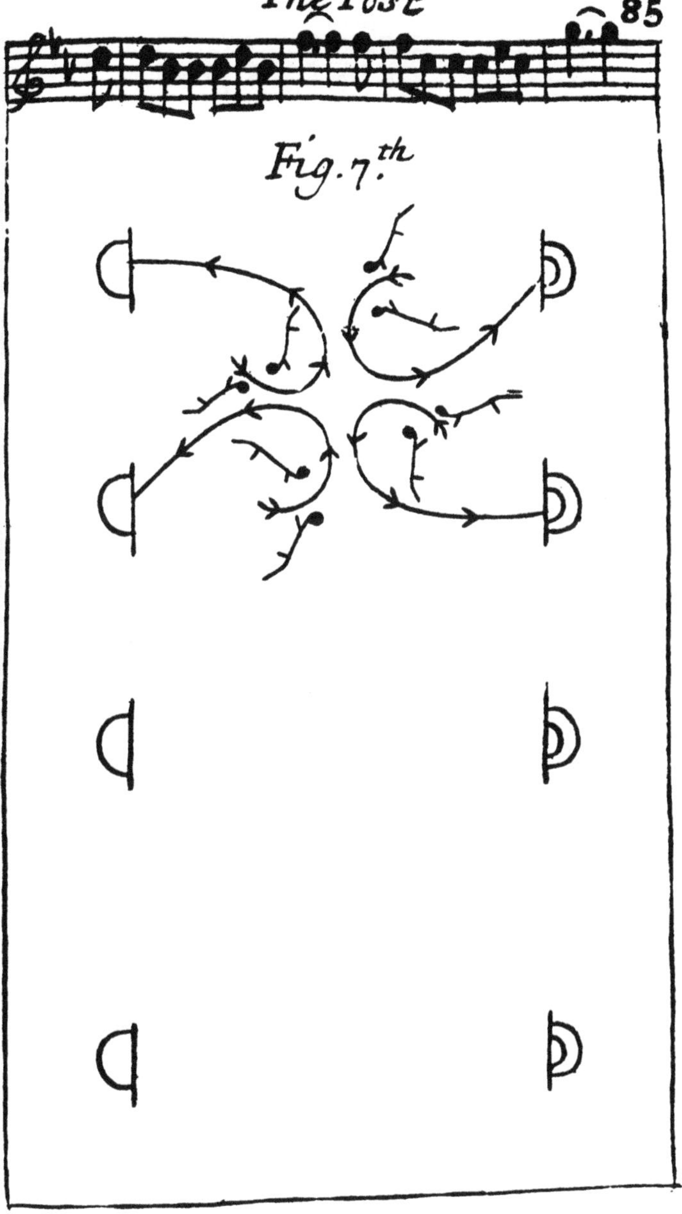

Fig. 7.th

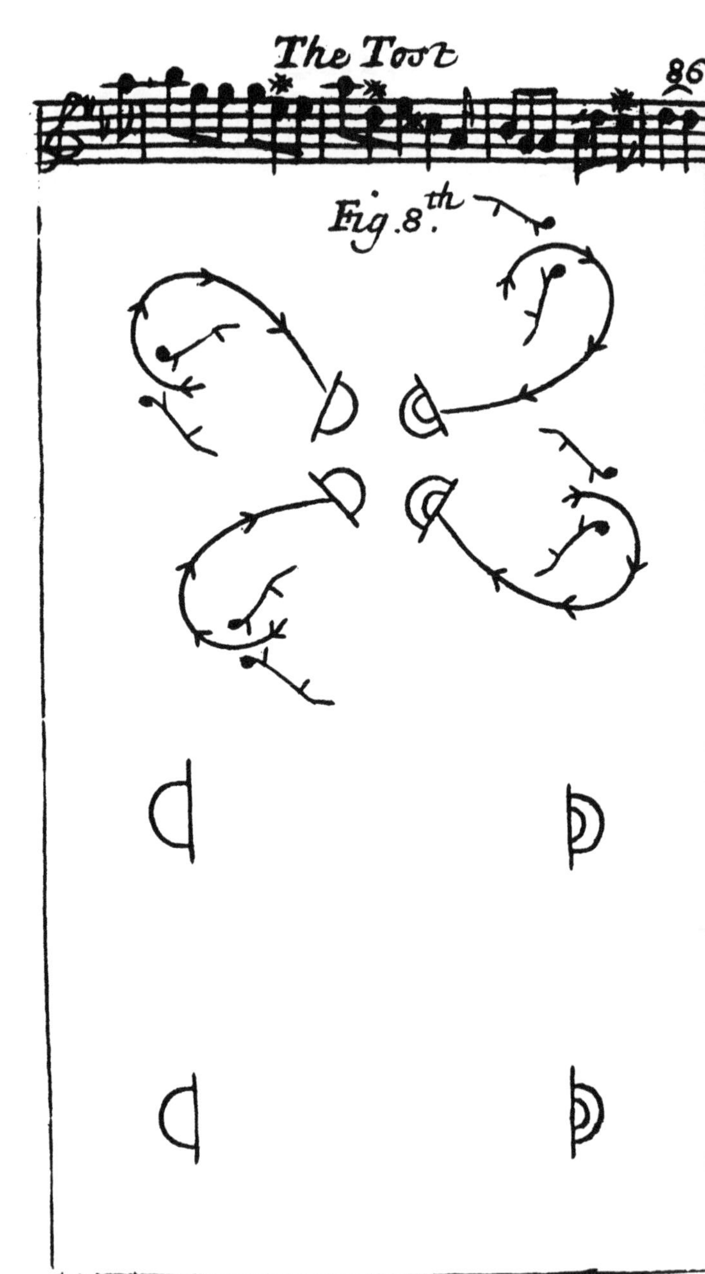
The Tost
Fig. 8.th

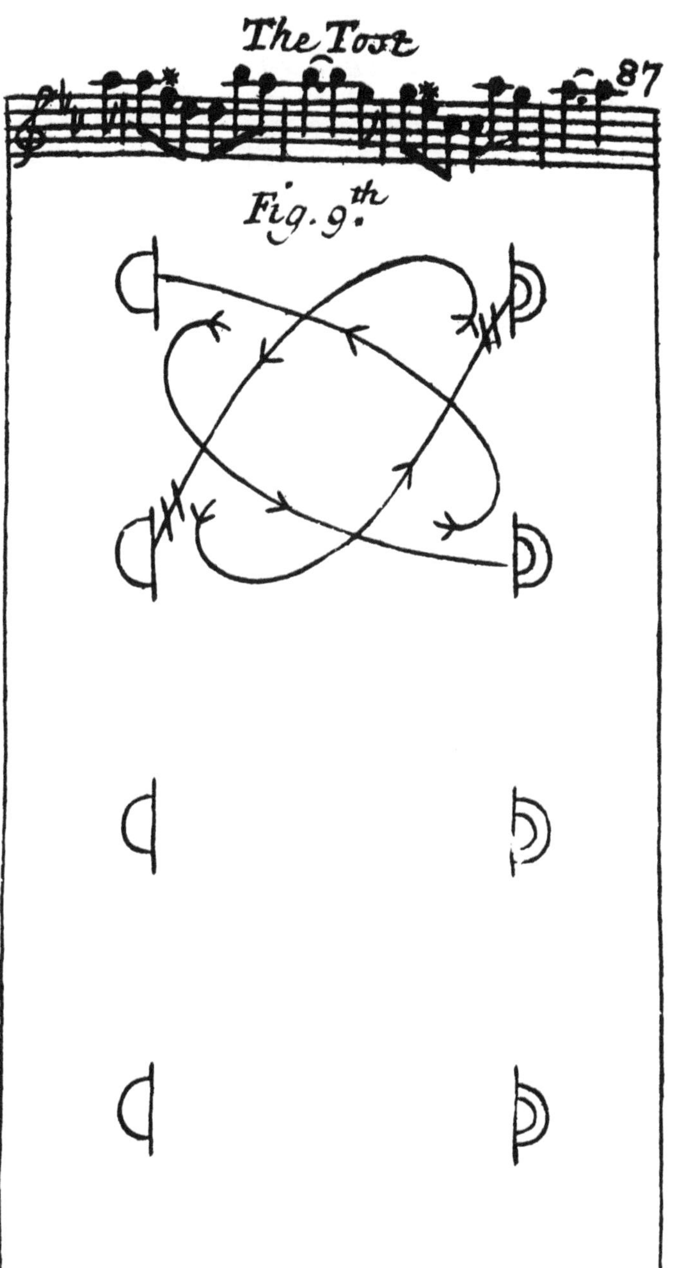
The Tost
Fig. 9th

The Tost

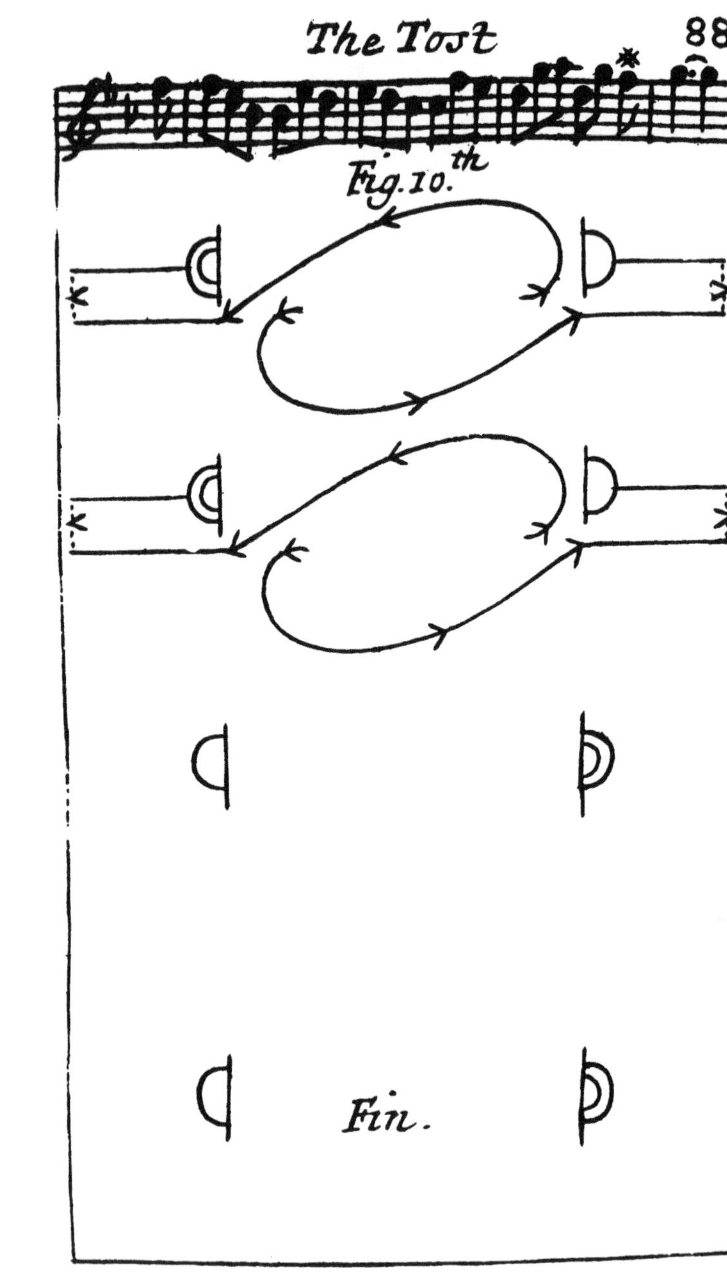

www.ingramcontent.com/pod-product-compliance
Ingram Content Group UK Ltd.
Pitfield, Milton Keynes, MK11 3LW, UK
UKHW041822290726
14061UKWH00003BA/144